You Are Worth Fighting For

You Are Worth Fighting For

YOUR GUIDE TO FINDING MENTAL WELLNESS AND SELF-LOVE

IVY WATTS, MPH

Copyright © 2022 by Ivy Watts Speaks

Cover Design: Tri Widyatmaka
Interior Design: Honeylette Pino
Editor: Jessica Gang
Cover Photography: Molly Greeley

All rights reserved. No part of this publication may be reproduced, used, performed, stored in a retrieval system, or transmitted in any form or by any means, electronic, mechanical, photocopying, recording or otherwise without the prior written permission of the author, Ivy Watts, if living, except for the critical articles or reviews.

Disclaimer:

The contents of this book are for informational purposes only and are not intended to be a substitute for professional psychological advice, diagnosis, or treatment. Always seek the advice of your physician, therapist, or other qualified health providers with any questions you may have regarding your mental health, mental condition, medical condition or treatment plan. Never disregard professional mental or medical advice or delay in seeking it because of something you have read on or through this book. If you need immediate assistance, please call 911 immediately, your local hospital, the National Suicide Prevention Lifeline (988) or text "Hello" to the Crisis Text line (741741).

If you would like to purchase bulk copies of *You Are Worth Fighting For*, contact Ivy Watts at ivy@ivywattsspeaks.com for discount pricing.

1st edition, October 2022

ISBN- 979-8-9868038-0-7

Printed in the United States of America

Dedication

In memory of my beautiful mother, Sang Watts.
February 7, 1954 - May 19, 2021

Mom, thank you for always believing in me and encouraging me for years to write a book. I finally did it, all in honor of you. The first person I wanted to call when I finished writing was you, and it pains me to know you'll never read this book, but you inspired *every word*. I miss you forever, my love will never change, and I love you, more.

Nothing Less Than a Bath and A Half
-Your most famous saying lives on, Momma

INTRODUCTION	1
CHAPTER 1: YOU ARE GOOD ENOUGH TO GO AFTER WHAT YOU DESERVE	7
Lesson One From My Mom: "Nothing Less Than A Bath And A Half"	
CHAPTER 2: YOU ARE STRONGER THAN YOU THINK	19
Lesson Two From My Mom: "I Can Do Bad All By Myself"	
CHAPTER 3: LOVE YOURSELF HOW YOU LOVE OTHERS	31
Lesson Three From My Mom: "Look At Yourself As a Third Person and Ask Yourself: 'Is This Good For Me?'"	
CHAPTER 4: GROWTH HAPPENS OUTSIDE OF YOUR COMFORT ZONES	41
Lesson Four From My Mom: "Don't Be Sorry, Be Conscious"	

CHAPTER 5: THERE IS STRENGTH IN FEELING YOUR FEELINGS - IT'S OKAY TO NOT BE OKAY   51
Lesson Five From My Mom: "It's Better To Be Pissed Off, Than To Be Pissed On"

CHAPTER 6: YOU ARE MORE THAN YOUR TO-DO LIST - HOW TO TAKE CARE OF YOUR MENTAL HEALTH   63
Lesson Six From My Mom (Part 1): "Take Care Of Those Teeth!"
Lesson Six From My Mom (Part 2): "Don't Be A Superhero"

CHAPTER 7: CREATING A SELF-CARE ROUTINE   81
Lesson Seven From My Mom: "Organization Is the Key To Life"

CHAPTER 8: FINDING LIGHT WITHIN THE DARKNESS AND KEEPING HOPE ALIVE   89
Lesson Eight From My Mom: "Keep Positive"

CHAPTER 9: YOU ARE A BEAUTIFUL WORK IN PROGRESS   101
Lesson Nine From My Mom: "Pack Your Patience"

CHAPTER 10: EVEN WHEN YOU FEEL LOST, YOU CAN ALWAYS FIND YOURSELF AGAIN   109
Lesson Ten From My Mom: "A Place For Everything And Everything In Its Place"

CHAPTER 11: KEEP MOVING FORWARD   115
Lesson Eleven From My Mom And Her Final Reminder: "This Too Shall Pass"

APPENDIX 121
ACKNOWLEDGEMENTS 125
ABOUT THE AUTHOR 129

Introduction

Sept 12, 2019, was a day that I will never forget and was one of the hardest days of my life. That was the day that my mom, my best friend, Sang Watts, let me know that the doctors suspected what I had a gut feeling about for months, that she had cancer, which we would soon find out was pancreatic cancer. For the next 651 long and hard days, she fought with a positivity and strength that I have never seen before.

    Throughout her journey with cancer, I developed an even stronger appreciation for my mom and all she was to me and to others. My mom had a lot of sayings that she said over, and over, and over again. When I was growing up, I didn't think too much into these statements, but during the year and a half that she battled cancer, I was able to reflect on a deeper level about all that she taught me. At the surface, some of her sayings were just reminding me to stay organized or to be patient in traffic, but as I've grown and reflected, I've realized that her sayings have a deeper meaning for finding self-love and self-worth.

My mom had a way about her where she was able to share exactly what was on her mind and still have it well received. She may not have always told someone what they wanted to hear, but she told them what they needed to hear in a way that was still compassionate and open for further discussion. I often look back in awe at her strength, her honesty, and her ability to stand up for what she believed in.

I wish I had connected my mom's teachings to finding my self-worth and learning to love myself earlier in life, as it would have helped me through the mental health challenges that I faced, but those challenges have made me who I am today. Today, I am thankful to share my story and tools for wellness as a Mental Health Empowerment Speaker and as a mental health advocate. I am a former DII All-American track athlete and a NCAA Woman of the Year Award finalist. In my personal life, I am a single mother to my beautiful baby girl, Charlotte, a daughter, and a friend to many. I am determined, loving, hardworking, and strive every day to reach my goals. I am someone who struggled to find my self-worth and who struggled with my mental health in silence, despite my accomplishments.

In our society, we are often encouraged to feel bad about ourselves, compare ourselves to others or even put ourselves down for not reaching our goals or for not meeting someone else's expectations, and this can easily lead to many of us struggling with our mental health. It's so easy to let the negativity that creeps into our minds completely cloud out any of the positives about ourselves or the situation. It's so easy to learn to grasp onto self-hate and self-criticism, than to learn to embrace the journey of self-love and compassionate growth. If you've ever felt like you weren't good enough, or that you weren't worthy of being in

INTRODUCTION

a certain situation, it's okay, society has conditioned you to feel this way, and you aren't alone. But what I hope you realize from this book is that you don't have to always feel that way. You don't have to feel stuck, because you aren't. There is a world of potential inside you that involves a life of acceptance, compassion, love, and joy from others and from yourself.

This book keeps my mother's legacy alive. On May 19, 2021, we lost my mom to pancreatic cancer. My mother was the most beautiful person I have ever known, and her strength lives on within me. The chapters that you are about to read aim to help you find your strength as well. The fear, grief, love, laughter, and moments of hope that came from my mom's journey throughout her life, my childhood, and her fight with cancer, influenced this book and the words that follow. This book is a compilation of eleven of my mom's teachings, each of which I have applied to this book with my own mental health lens, to help you find your own sense of mental wellness, self-worth, and self-love. Each chapter of this book mirrors a saying my mom said to us all of the time when we were growing up, that with my own reflection and growth, have molded me into the person I am today. Through the tools and reflection prompts/questions provided, you'll walk away not only with some new catchy phrases, but also a renewed sense of self and you'll learn to love and accept yourself for who you are and know that in this moment and in every moment, you are more than good enough.

I can still so clearly hear her saying each and every single one of her famous sayings and I know she would be so happy that I am sharing her teachings with all of you. I can see her smiling now, so proud of me for writing this book, and so very proud of you for picking it up and choosing to do something powerful for you. Let's dive in!

Trigger warning* - This book discusses mental health challenges including anxiety, depression, disordered eating, suicidal ideation, and relationship abuse. This book also discusses a challenging cancer journey. Please know if you are experiencing any of these challenges, you are not alone and help is always available. If at any point these topics become too much or too triggering for you, please take a moment to take care of yourself and return back to the book after you've given yourself a chance to reset. Please know that if you need support, you can reach out to resources such as the Crisis Text Line (Text "Hello" to 741741) or the National Suicide Prevention Lifeline (Dial 988) at any time, 24/7. There are also additional resources listed in the appendix at the end of this book. Help is always available.

Lesson One

FROM MY MOM

"Nothing Less Than A Bath And A Half"

CHAPTER

YOU ARE GOOD ENOUGH TO GO AFTER WHAT YOU DESERVE

I want you to think back to when you were a child. You were probably fearless. You probably had big dreams to be a teacher, an astronaut, and a professional athlete and believed wholeheartedly that you could reach all those dreams. You probably took risks and weren't afraid if you didn't get things right on the first try. You probably weren't worried about what others thought about you. Somewhere along the way, we lose that fearlessness, and we begin to question ourselves, our ability, and our worth on this earth. Somewhere along the way, we stop believing in ourselves and become full of doubt that our goals are even in reach. Somewhere along the way, we forget the light we add to the world, just by being who we are.

This mindset often halts us in our path toward our future and makes us feel that we are not worthy of doing the things we want to do. In turn, we settle. We settle for relationships, friendships, jobs and experiences that are not good for us because we are afraid we will never find anything better. Simply, we settle into the belief that we are not good enough. I fell into that belief for most of my life. I lived most of my life feeling like I was not good enough and I settled for a lot of people and situations that only made me feel more worthless than I already felt. My mom did her best to empower me to believe in myself and go after my dreams, but the pressure from society for me to be perfect led me down an opposing path.

My mom was always someone who believed she could reach her goals and one of those goals led to the creation of her signature phrase, "Nothing less than a bath and a half." A phrase I heard countless times throughout my childhood and adult life. If you knew my mom, you knew how important it was to her to have more than one bathroom in her home. My mother grew up in Oxford, Mississippi, where she shared one small home with six siblings and her mother. In the first home they lived in, they had a single outhouse to use as their bathroom. The next home she lived in with her siblings was a step above their last situation, now having a bathroom inside of the house, but only a curtain served as a door to the bathroom. My mom spent the rest of her life sharing just one bathroom with other people in her home. She met my father while in college in Mississippi and they eventually settled in Waltham, Massachusetts, in a three-bedroom, one bathroom home. My mom thought this living arrangement was only temporary, but it ended up being the home where they would raise both my brother and I. My mom continued to share one bathroom with all of us. This proved to be a challenge, especially during our teenage years, as there was always a fight over who got to shower and get ready first. Every week my mom would play scratch tickets, hoping she would get her lucky break that would allow her to

CHAPTER 1 | *LESSON ONE*

afford the dream she had been craving, and finally add on that half bath.

Since we grew up being told to have "nothing less than a bath and a half," almost every day, both my brother and I knew that any home we ever purchased would never get a Sang Watts approval without having at least a bath and a half in it. I even have a sign in my half bathroom at my house with this signature saying (photo below), and I tell all my friends when they are house hunting about the sheer importance of that half bath.

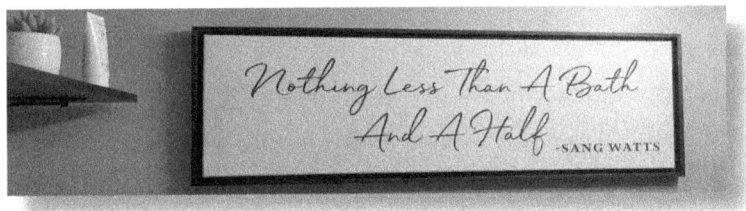

It happened quite frequently that my mom would be getting ready to leave the house and needed something in the bathroom and whenever it was occupied, she would mutter, "Nothing less..." Before she could even finish her sentence, one of us would finish for her, "We know, Mom, nothing less than a bath and a half." I can see her clearly now raising her thumb to show her excitement that we understood, but also sharing with us a gentle eye roll, while she impatiently waited her turn in the bathroom. I like to think about her saying that phrase over and over as more than just an important logistical part of life and living situations. I like to think that by constantly reminding us to have more than just one bathroom, she was teaching us to find our worth and that we should never settle for anything less than we deserve. My mom's signature saying of, "Nothing less than a bath and a half," is a lesson and reminder for us all to find our worth and not settle.

My mom never got her bath and a half, but she never stopped trying. And just like when she found out about her cancer diagnosis, she refused to settle and stop fighting even when several doctors told her early on that she would eventually pass away from this awful disease. Early on in her fight, my mom said to us, "I plan to fight and beat this cancer. Right now, this cancer is just a part of me, and I have no intention of letting it stick around and letting it become my friend." My mother was determined to not settle for the awful statistics around pancreatic cancer. She could have heard the statistics and decided she wasn't going to fight to live, but my mother knew she was deserving of having a beautiful and happy life, so she fought, and fought, and fought. **My mom knew that she was worth fighting for.** Through countless rounds of chemo, radiation, a major surgery, additional radiation, so many hugs, lots of disappointing news, hospital stays, and traumatic experiences, my mom rarely lost her smile or her strength and positivity.

My mom's fight inspires me to this day to not settle and to know that I have the tools and strength within me to reach my goals. From her journey, I learned that even when you put your best self into something and you stay positive and do all of the things you need to do to succeed, things don't always go how we want them to go. Unfortunately, despite my mom fighting as hard as she did, her fight only lasted just shy of two years before she passed. My mom didn't get the end goal that she had for herself which was to continue to live a life of joy. But I want all of us to remember that just because our journey may not go how we anticipate it to go, that doesn't mean our journey isn't worth living. I

CHAPTER 1 | *LESSON ONE*

challenge you to make a conscious choice today to be your best self and to go after what you want in this world. We learn so much about ourselves in the process if we choose to go after the very goal that scares us and to know that no matter what the outcome is, we are worthy of trying.

What parts of your life have you felt yourself settle? What areas of your life did you think you didn't deserve to have, so you took a less appealing journey instead? Are you settling for a relationship that doesn't grow you, serve you or make you happy? Are you settling for a job that will pay you less than you deserve? Are you applying to a college that feels like a safe choice, because someone has told you that you aren't capable of going to your dream school? Are you settling for a friendship that feels comfortable, even though you have both grown and your values no longer align? How many times have you looked back with regret on the decisions you made, knowing you should have advocated for yourself and gotten a different result? How many times have you let fear keep you from trying a new skill or reaching toward a new goal? The answer to some of these questions may be unsettling and make you feel disappointed in your life choices and maybe even in yourself. It's okay if you have settled before in the past, but know that you can start today to take risks, show up for yourself, and create the life you have dreamed of.

My first challenge for you is to write down what two to three goals you have for yourself, what two to three things hold you back from achieving those goals, what two to three mindset shifts you need to make to adjust what is holding you back, and what two to three steps you can take today to get closer to reaching those goals. For example, perhaps your goal is to run a 5k by the end of the year and the fear that you are not strong or fit enough

//

to finish keeps you from training in the first place. To shift your mindset, you could recognize that your fear is a valid fear, but remind yourself that your body is stronger than you give yourself credit for, and that you have the tools and strength within you to begin training and run the race, even if that means you take a few breaks or don't run as fast as you'd like. The first step you can take today is to walk a 5k and get your body used to that length of distance. The more that we take the space to rewire our brains away from our fears, and the more that we take a step toward our goal, no matter how small, we can see that although that first step can be scary, it will be worth it, rather than living with the feelings of regret or sadness for never taking that first step at all.

 I settled for most of my life and I was too afraid of what it meant to find my worth. I will forever be grateful for my journey and what it taught me, but I think about how I could have learned to love and forgive myself through the process if I had found self-love and self-worth earlier. I think about how I would have gotten closer to reaching my goals, had I chosen to invest in myself and what I deserved. I always felt out of place growing up. I can still vividly remember the feelings I had walking into Kennedy Middle School every day. I remember being bullied that I wasn't "Black enough," and I internalized that remark early on to mean that I wasn't good enough. I remember I felt such deep shame bringing my own lunch to school, because none of my Black peers brought their own lunch. I would hold my lunch behind my back, hoping that by doing so, I would experience less judgment. Although the judgment from others hurt, it was the judgment I had about myself that created the deepest pain. From an early age, I hated who I was and wanted to change everything about myself. Growing up, I believed the stigma that exists around

CHAPTER 1 | *LESSON ONE*

mental health, so when society, family, and friends told me that if I talked about what I was feeling, I would be labeled as weak, I believed them. It is this very stigma that keeps many of us from talking about what we are going through, for fear of being judged or labeled as weak, so instead we struggle in silence.

These feelings of self-hate and low self-esteem from such a young age turned into a crippling anxiety that I never felt I could talk about. My struggle in silence continued throughout high school and college. I ran track my entire life and truly began to feel the pressure to be perfect during my high school track career. My desire to be perfect came directly from feeling like I wasn't good enough. I told myself that I needed to be perfect on and off the track in order to be loved, appreciated and respected. I told myself that if I wasn't perfect, that I would be a failure. My belief that talking about your mental health was a sign of weakness only magnified in the athletic culture. In the athletic world, you are expected to put on your jersey and tie up your spikes and basically mask the pain you are feeling. The term, "suck it up" is thrown around constantly. The pressure to be perfect only magnified when I continued my track career at University of New Haven, a Division II college. While at New Haven, I continuously pushed aside the anxiety and depression I was feeling, deeming it as insignificant, yet I was in mental anguish. I didn't know who I was, I hated the way I looked, I hated that I felt like I was always falling short, and I hated that no matter what I did, I always spoke negatively about myself.

I became obsessed with running 54 seconds in the 400 meter dash, my main event. There was a lot of pressure on me from my coaches and teammates to try and run this "perfect" time. I spoke about 54 seconds every chance I could. I dreamed about it,

I trained hard for it and I was on track to run it in a race. What I didn't realize was holding me back was my lack of self-worth and my negative self-talk. The memories of being in the blocks before a race are palpable; I can still smell the smoke of the race gun going off right after the official said his commands, "Runners take your mark, get set." Simultaneously, I remember my heart would drop and all I would hear was the anxiety that overtook me. "I can't do this, I'm not good enough." The whole race, I would put myself down again, and again, and again. I was trying so hard to meet everyone else's expectations, that I was losing myself further. Every time I did not run 54 seconds, I felt more and more like a failure. I tried to do everything possible to change what I was eating and what my body looked like so that I could meet this "perfect goal." After my coaches put me on countless diets and constantly checked our weight at practice, I began struggling with disordered eating patterns, which only further fueled my self-hate and created a lifetime of body image struggles.

No one knew how much I was struggling mentally. People only saw that I was this perfect student and perfect athlete, because that's what I worked so hard for everyone to see. I graduated from college with Summa Cum Laude honors (3.97 GPA). I was All-American in the 4x400, the Distinguished Student-Athlete Scholar two years in a row, and named Woman of the Year for the Northeast-10 Conference and a Top 30 Finalist for the NCAA Woman of the Year award. After college, I felt like I lost my identity as an athlete, I was in an emotionally abusive relationship, and had fully lost myself. I began spiraling into a depressive state with thoughts of not wanting to be here anymore. It took me a few years after college before I was able to finally begin my journey to find my bath and a half and to find my worth and not settle for less than I deserved. My journey included starting therapy to heal the anxiety and depression I had struggled with in silence for so many years. Therapy became an avenue for me to begin taking risks to find out who I was outside of the external factors of track and relationships that I used to define me. Therapy allowed me to find my voice and to know that my story had meaning and value. I finally began to practice self-love and learned the power of positive affirmations to rewire the years of negativity that had encapsulated my life. Through consistent hard work, I was able to see that I could stand up for myself and what I believed in and that I could say no to opportunities that were not good for me and truly go after what I deserved. I was finally able to love and accept myself for me and only let people and opportunities into my life who challenged me to grow and who loved me for who I was on the journey.

You do not have to wait until someone says that your struggle is "bad enough" or until you feel all hope is gone, to start your own journey of healing. For my mom's entire life, she had to wait her turn to use the bathroom, but you don't have to wait for your turn to begin your journey of seeking out your worth. I wish I had started my journey of healing and learning my self-worth sooner instead of letting the stigma of mental health keep me from seeking the help I needed. You truly can start today, no matter how frightening the journey ahead may seem. Finding your self-worth means knowing that you are good enough, knowing that you are worthy of showing up as you are, knowing that you are strong, and knowing that you don't have to settle just because it feels like the safe choice. You are worthy of going after what you deserve. Use the experiences of your past to fuel your future and know that what you may have settled for in the past, you do not have to settle for now. Use what you have learned to carry you forward. Choose to not let the disappointments or challenges from your past dictate what happens in your future. The next time you have an opportunity that you are unsure you are capable of completing, I challenge you to remember that you have the tools within you, and you can reframe your mindset to see that you deserve more and that you are truly worth this journey of finding your own sense of a bath and a half.

Lesson Two

FROM MY MOM

"I Can Do Bad All By Myself"

CHAPTER 2

YOU ARE STRONGER THAN YOU THINK

We live in a world where perfection is often expected. If you aren't getting perfect grades or if you don't have the perfect relationship, you and others may think that you are a failure. The tricky thing about seeking out perfection, is that you will always fall short; because, what truly is perfection? Your idea of perfection is going to be much different than my idea of perfection. Even if you have a goal for yourself and you meet it "perfectly," there is always going to be another goal that you set for yourself that can make you feel like you could have or should have done more. In your search for perfection, you may fixate on the one thing that didn't go quite perfectly, and that can make you feel hopeless and terrible about yourself. Seeking out perfection only makes us feel bad about ourselves because perfection is unattainable, especially if we are comparing ourselves to other people in our lives or the people we see on social media.

This perfectionist mindset that makes us feel bad about ourselves often leads us to seek out validation in every aspect of our lives. From a young age, we begin to crave external validation. In kindergarten, I remember getting stickers for doing a good job and among many other things in life, this is a reward given by someone else. If we do not feel like we are good enough, we are going to seek out someone who validates our existence. Or even worse, we are going to seek out someone who puts us down even more than we already do to ourselves, because we feel that is what we deserve. The early desire and need for someone else to praise us and the neglect of praising ourselves becomes a vicious cycle of self-doubt and anxiety and keeps us from living a life where we recognize our worth.

My mom was one of the strongest people I've ever had the opportunity to know, and her ability to validate herself, rather than seek it out from others, was always inspiring. Many people remember my mom through the strength she showed during her fight with pancreatic cancer, a fight where her internal validation of her strength kept her going. My mom had always told me challenging stories about her life that demonstrated her strength, and to see her thriving despite it all, was always remarkable. I remember my mom telling me about her first husband, before she met my dad, and although she did not tell me all of the details, she did tell me that she was a victim of abuse. One thing that I remember her saying about her journey in this relationship was that at some point along the way she realized she deserved better and was worthy of more than what she had and that, quite frankly, she could do bad all by herself. That realization, her strong sense of self-worth and her strength, allowed her to leave that relationship and begin her own healing journey.

CHAPTER 2 | *LESSON TWO*

    I remember feeling so stuck in an emotionally abusive relationship and not realizing that I had the same strength deep within me to put myself first, just as my mom did all those years ago. I am not sure exactly where my intense desire to be loved and accepted began, but all I know is that it was all consuming. I sought out love and acceptance for all of the wrong reasons. I wanted that love and acceptance, because I couldn't love or accept myself. I craved the world to see me as perfect, just so I could receive validation that I was doing a good job. How could I ever do bad all by myself, if I couldn't even stand the thought of truly being by myself? So instead, I chose to stay in a relationship that broke me, made me feel worthless and only increased my desire for external validation and love, rather than seeking it out from myself. At the core of my existence was the need for external validation, it felt like if I didn't have it, I wouldn't survive. I couldn't fathom the idea of being alone or learning how to accept myself so year after year, fight after fight, disappointment after disappointment, I stayed in a relationship that I should have left. I stayed because in between the tears, there were laughs that made the tears and the fights seem not so bad. I stayed because I became dependent on another person to bring happiness into my life, because I didn't know how to do that on my own. So I stayed, and I stayed, until I couldn't stay anymore. Finally, I found the inner strength that I'd had all along and realized it was time for me to walk away, and to finally be bad all by myself.

    The day that I walked away from years of a toxic relationship with someone else and also a toxic, negative relationship with myself, was one of the scariest days of my life, but I was also so relieved. I had finally been set free of the chains that had been holding me back for so long. I finally had permission to be me, to be unapologetically Ivy. But because I had depended on someone else for so long to give meaning to who Ivy was, I had no idea who the girl staring back at me in the mirror was. I was determined to find out, though, no matter what it took, to redefine who Ivy was and who she wanted to be. It took me too long to realize that the acceptance I craved my entire life needed to come from the very person staring back at me in the mirror–I finally realized that it needed to be me and not someone else that made me feel worthy for simply being me. Driving home from that momentous day, I left the past behind me with every mile and drove forward into a new life, one where I could be bad all by myself, but also surrounded by the support of those who truly loved me and were going to help me on this new journey.

Being bad all by yourself and finding your self-worth is making the hard, yet right, decision of leaving a bad situation and learning to be okay with being on your own and not dependent on someone else for your worth. In my journey of healing, a friend shared this quote with me by Warsan Shire, "My alone feels so good, I'll only have you if you are sweeter than my solitude." I was able to truly learn to love being around myself and only chose to invite people into my life who added to the happiness I was finally able to create for myself. I challenge you to also choose to surround yourself with people who only add to your life and not those who take from it. I encourage you to choose to learn to love yourself so much with all of your beautiful, imperfect traits that make you, you. Learning to love yourself and seeking out validation from yourself, and not others, is one of the most beautiful feelings. Even though you can do bad all by yourself, you aren't alone on this journey. I am here with you every day, continually navigating my own journey of self-love and validation after years of self-hate. You have support and love around you to help you through this challenge. Even if your voice is speaking loudly that no one is here for you, or no one will understand, there are always people out there who want to help you navigate your challenge, and help empower you to continue to add light to your life.

Maybe you have found yourself in a similar situation as myself or my mom. Maybe, you have struggled with figuring out who you are and what you are truly capable of without someone or something in your life. Maybe you depend on another individual, be it your partner, friend, relative, or coach, to bring you happiness. Maybe you don't think you are good enough or beautiful enough so in turn, you don't feel confident and you crave external validation from whoever will give it to you, even if they bring you down. Maybe you are in a relationship or situation that you know deep down, you would be better off without, but you are afraid of what will be on the other side of walking away. That fear is an incredibly valid fear. But on the other side of that fear, is a world of possibility where you can create your own happiness, where you can feel good enough as you are in this very moment, where you can know that you have made mistakes, but that those mistakes don't dictate your future or your worth. On the other side of fear is a world where you can learn to validate yourself and have external validation be something that makes you feel good, but not something that you feel like you need to survive.

To learn how to validate yourself, your accomplishments, your strengths and how far you have come, take a moment and reflect on at least five challenges you have experienced in your life. These challenges can be big or small. Try to remember how you felt when you were experiencing those challenges. Were you afraid? Angry? Disappointed? Now think about the challenges where you felt so broken, that it almost felt impossible to continue on. Maybe this was a time when you didn't want to show your face at school ever again because you were mortified about your performance at a talent show, or maybe this was a time that you experienced a break up and the pain was so overwhelming that you didn't think you could get through the day. But despite the fear and the pain, you showed up and got through the day. *You showed back up-yes, you.* Despite the odds, your inner strength proved to you and the world that you are so much stronger than you think. You have gotten through challenges and you have preserved and continued to move forward. You have shown that you can do bad all by yourself and that you don't need the negativity from others, but that you are so incredibly worthy of a world of positivity. I want you to write down these challenges and how you overcame them and keep them in an accessible spot, such as the notes in your phone, and come back to these moments when you are feeling like you can't get through a new challenge. Use these past challenges to remind yourself that you can get through this new challenge, because you've overcome challenges in the past, and you can do it again, and again, and again. You have all of the tools within you. My coach used to say to us before a meet, "You have already done the work, now it is time to perform." You have already experienced challenges and have done the hard work of navigating those challenges and through them you grew in strength and resiliency. As you move forward, you can take what you have learned, and the tools and strength you already have within you, to work through any new challenge or obstacle. Believe in yourself to work through this challenge and know that all hope is not lost. When you can begin to validate yourself and your ideas, you will be able to see that you do not need to depend on others for that validation, because you will have done the work to know that who you are in this moment is worthy of receiving all of the good coming your way.

It can be hard to feel proud of ourselves for our growth when we are constantly told by society that who we are isn't good enough or that we need to be "perfect." It is easy to overlook even your smallest accomplishments and focus only on the areas where you could be doing better. But I want to challenge you today to celebrate how far you have come. Even if it doesn't feel like you have come far, you are doing something right now and challenging yourself in some way that your past self would have never done. Maybe even reading this book on mental health is something you would have never done before in the past. Maybe you have been struggling to get out of bed, but you did it today. Or maybe you have been struggling with disliking your body and it has been hard to look in the mirror, but today you gave yourself a small compliment. Progress is progress. No matter how big or small. I want you to celebrate you, because you deserve to be celebrated. When you begin to celebrate yourself, you begin to validate yourself for your accomplishments and cheer yourself on, rather than always waiting for someone else to do it. Celebrating and validating yourself is a vital step in your self-love journey. You deserve to recognize that you have overcome so much, and you are still here today, fighting and pushing. In your darkest of times, remind yourself of how far you have come. Remind yourself of your growth and always, always remember, that who you are is more than good enough. I celebrate you for all that you are doing today that once felt impossible. Both my mom and I took steps in our lives that felt impossible, but ended up being the steps that changed our lives for the better, and the step my mom took all those years ago developed the strength she needed to tackle cancer years later.

Taking the first step into the journey of finding your self-worth will involve a lot of ups and downs, including learning how to be okay with being yourself. Always remember that you have the power, don't let someone else take it from you. You can walk away from people or situations that bring you down and do bad all by yourself. For so long in my life, I let someone else take my power. I let someone else dictate what was good for me and what wasn't. I had no self-worth, so I sought it out in someone else, but by doing so, I lost myself even more, and I lost my power to control who I was, what I wanted and where I was headed. I'm reminded often about how different my life is right now. How much more often I feel wrapped in love and acceptance from others but more importantly from myself. At one point in my life, I never thought I would get to this place. I never thought I would be able to take my power back, reclaim who Ivy is, and finally recognize my worth. But I did, and you can, too, you can learn to validate yourself, learn to love yourself, stay true to who you are despite what others think, and recognize your strength to keep moving forward.

When I finally left my emotionally abusive relationship, my mom gave me a poem that was helpful for her when she started her own journey of self-worth and self-love. This journey truly is about knowing that you can provide love to yourself and that the validation and acceptance you are craving from others, can also come from you. When you begin to love and nourish yourself, you will be surprised at all the love and positivity that flows your way, naturally. What you put out into the world, you begin to receive.

CHAPTER 2 | *LESSON TWO*

This poem still centers me to this day, I hope it does the same for you.

"Comes The Dawn" by Veronica Shoffstall:

"After a while you learn the subtle difference between holding a hand and chaining a soul. And you learn that love doesn't mean leaning and company doesn't mean security. And you begin to understand that kisses aren't contracts and presents aren't promises. And you begin to accept your defeats with your head held high and your eyes open with the grace of an adult and not the grief of a child. You learn to build your roads on today because tomorrow's ground is too uncertain for plans and futures have a way of falling down mid flight. After a while you learn that even sunshine burns if you get too much. So you plant your own garden and decorate your own soul, instead of waiting for someone to bring you flowers. And you learn that you really can endure, that you really are strong and that you really do have worth. And you learn and you learn, and you learn. With every goodbye you learn."

After reading this poem, ask yourself what it means to you in your current situation and what you might learn about yourself if you are able to say goodbye to someone or something that is no longer good for you. Think about how liberating it might be to plant your own garden and love yourself so deeply, despite all of your flaws. Think about how freeing it will be to learn to validate yourself and not depend on someone else to do it for you. Think about how incredible it will be to know your worth so deeply that you only invite those into your life who uplift you. As you reflect, know that in the future, when inevitable struggles come, that you are stronger than you think, that you have the tools within you and that you can be empowered to water your own soul and know you can endure all that will come your way. Remember that I am here with you and some days I can lose sight of loving and validating myself, especially on my grieving journey. Just like you, I am picking up the pieces and putting myself together one by one. We are stronger than yesterday, we can take that first step that often feels impossible so we can lead a better life. Just like my mom, we don't need to depend on others for validation because we can love ourselves as we are and do bad all by ourselves.

Lesson Three

FROM MY MOM

"Look At Yourself As a Third Person and Ask Yourself: 'Is This Good For Me?'"

CHAPTER 3

LOVE YOURSELF HOW YOU LOVE OTHERS

This saying of my mom's was by far the most frustrating one because I wasn't ready to hear it. It took me a long time to feel ready to leave the emotionally abusive relationship that I was in, because of my lack of self-worth. My mom knew, from early on, that the relationship I was in wasn't healthy for me. She tried over and over to get me to leave, wanting me to see that I deserved better, but I had to have my own journey, to finally see what she saw. She would always say to me, "Ivy, look at yourself as a third person," and I can still feel how much those simple words got under my skin! I wasn't capable of looking at myself as a third person. My mom was asking me to look at myself as someone looking from the outside in or to look at myself as a friend who was in the same position as I was, and to ask myself, what would that person looking in say about my relationship, or what would I say to a friend who was in a relationship like mine.

When I think about this lesson, I think about how we need to love and treat ourselves the way we love and treat others. How many times have you given someone incredible, life changing advice, but you walk away and do the exact opposite thing you told them to do? I know many of us are guilty of doing exactly that. We can give the best advice, but we struggle to take it for ourselves. How many times have you shown up for other people, but not shown up for yourself? How many times have you complimented others but not been able to compliment yourself? How many times have you shown compassion to others, but were unable to show compassion to yourself for the same situation? Does any of this sound familiar to your own life? We can easily show up for others in our lives. We pour from our own cup and constantly help others, without thinking about filling our own cup and helping ourselves. We will clap and give a standing ovation for a friend, but for ourselves, we will shy away from even stepping on stage with the belief that we are not worthy of being in the room. It is a great trait to be able to see the good in others and be kind to them, but what about being kind to yourself? You deserve that same kindness and love that you so easily give to others.

I know exactly how it feels to show up for others, but do almost nothing for myself, to spread myself thin and put the needs of others above my own, and to love others but hate myself. I know how it feels to give compassion to others, but be angry at myself for not doing more. I felt this deeply when we received the news that my mom's cancer had progressed to stage four on March 31, 2021. I had already been struggling with depression throughout my mom's cancer journey, but the progression and the news that she had less than a year to live, really struck me at my core. When my mom passed away on May 19, 2021, less than two months after her cancer progressed, I lost key pieces of myself. I felt less motivated, I felt less joy, less excitement and less gratitude for life itself. Simple tasks became incredibly exhausting and difficult to complete. I spent a lot of time being really angry at the universe for making my mom so sick and taking her away from me. I still experience emotions of anger, sadness, but yet also feelings of calm that she is no longer in pain. But overall, I know I am forever different since she has been gone. It's easy to get angry with ourselves and be mean to ourselves in these emotional states. You may start asking yourself, "Why can't I do the things I used to do?" or you may be saying things like, "Stop being lazy." In those moments, we stop giving ourselves compassion and then the cycle of anger and sadness only grows deeper. My therapist constantly reminded me during this period of intense grief, that I experienced a huge life change with the loss of my best friend, and that I was going to have moments, days, weeks or months where I just would not feel motivated, because my body and mind were going through so much. I had to re-learn how to give myself compassion and be patient and kind to myself during my grieving journey.

Maybe right now you are angry or disappointed with yourself. Maybe you have experienced a huge loss and that is weighing you down. Or maybe you feel like you are losing yourself. Maybe you find yourself stuck in a situation that you know you shouldn't be in. I want us to channel seeing ourselves as a third person, no matter how frustrating or scary that might be to do. I want you to think about your current situation, and ask yourself, what would you tell a friend to do who was in the exact same situation, and then ask yourself, how might you be able to apply that same advice to your own life, starting today. I want you to ask yourself, how would you want a friend to be treated, and to know that you are worthy of that exact same treatment from yourself, to yourself and from others. You would likely never tell your best friend that they were ugly or fat or worthless, so why tell yourself those things? If you had a friend you were around all the time and they told you that you were worthless, would you want to keep that friend around? Probably not! At the end of the day, you have to spend more time with yourself than anyone in this world, so choose to be kind to yourself. Choose to be kind to the negative voices in your head and give yourself some compassion today: sleep in tomorrow morning or make time today to take a nap, eat your favorite comfort food, take a walk, talk to a friend, or do absolutely nothing at all and pause in the chaos of life to just be. Take a step away from your busy life to do something you enjoy. Don't let life pass you by without taking some time for you, make sure to do something nice for yourself for a change. During times of pain, it's important more than ever to give yourself, your mind and your body what you need.

Look At Yourself As A Third Person To Forgive Yourself

One of the biggest parts about being compassionate with yourself and loving yourself is forgiving yourself. It's so important to forgive yourself when you feel like you've fallen short, when you have made a mistake or said the wrong thing or even hurt someone unintentionally. It is so easy to beat ourselves up for the mistakes we have made because we receive so much pressure from others and ourselves, so when we make a mistake, it hurts more than we could have imagined. In these moments, it's so important to be kind to ourselves and remind ourselves that we are only human. Sometimes we will lash out at people who mean the most to us, sometimes we will say or do the wrong things, but that's okay. Life wouldn't be interesting if we always had it all together! Allow yourself to yell, scream and cry, and then allow yourself to recognize you are only human, surrounded by millions of other people who are making mistakes, too, and then give yourself permission to forgive yourself. It is okay to mess up. Although too often desired, it is unrealistic to never mess up in life. If you can acknowledge that you will make mistakes, and you can allow yourself to feel the frustration, sadness or disappointment, you can allow yourself to experience the beauty of self-compassion sooner. The people that love us the most will always forgive us when we mess up. We deserve to forgive ourselves as well. We deserve to love ourselves so much through those mistakes, that even when we feel like we didn't do our best, we can provide comfort and love to ourselves, rather than criticizing ourselves.

Look At Yourself As A Third Person To Love Yourself And Be Patient With Yourself

Self-love means continually finding space to practice kindness and patience toward yourself and learning to love your flaws and imperfections, even when society encourages you to talk negatively about yourself. Almost every time you go on your phone, you are receiving messages of some kind telling you to change who you are and what you look like, whether that be through an advertisement, or that fitness model you follow on Instagram telling you to not eat after 5 PM. It's no wonder we feel less than and unworthy when we are constantly comparing ourselves to these advertisements that promote unrealistic ideas of who we should be. In a world where society tells you to be anyone but you, I challenge you to take the most beautiful act of rebellion and go against society's pressures, and simply be you. You were put on this earth as you are for a reason. Why try to change who you are when the very thing that makes you beautiful is the fact that you are uniquely you? When you can start showing society that it will no longer win, that it will no longer have power over you, then you can begin to accept yourself. But self-love takes a lot of work, patience and perseverance, because you are fighting against the pressures of society every minute of every day. But I think that is what makes the self-love journey that much more beautiful and meaningful, because despite the odds, having self-love allows you to carry on and push forward.

When you learn to love yourself, it means doing your best to wake up every morning and be patient with yourself. I can never promise you that you will wake up every morning and love yourself or be proud of yourself, I know I don't. But when we can be patient with ourselves, we can accept that we will have bad days, and we can be compassionate to ourselves when we mess up or fall short. No matter where you are on this journey, choose patience and kindness every time. Know that you are worthy of giving yourself patience, kindness, compassion, acceptance and so much love. And no matter how difficult the journey may get, know that self-love is the greatest gift because not only have you embarked on the most beautiful journey, you have fought against society, and you have won.

CHAPTER 3 | *LESSON THREE*

Look At Yourself As A Third Person To Recognize Your Strength

I once saw a quote that read, "While you're being overly critical of yourself, someone is admiring your strength." (Author Unknown). As you look at yourself as a third person, I hope you know that there is someone out there looking in on your unique journey and sees your strength and feels proud to watch your growth. You truly are stronger than you realize, and so many people believe that about you. I believe that about you simply because you chose to pick up this book and learn how to love yourself through the pain you may be experiencing. Just like you would love your best friend through their pain and provide them with patience and acceptance, by picking up this book and learning how to take care of your mental wellness, you are also learning to love yourself with patience and acceptance. Despite you taking this step, I know it can still be hard to love ourselves through this journey, but try not to be so hard on yourself, try to see yourself as that third person and be kind to yourself.

- - - -

When I finally was able to look at myself as a third person, I was able to see how the untreated anxiety and self-hate I had was weighing me down, affecting my self-confidence and keeping me in a relationship that only made me feel worse about myself. I was able to finally reflect on where I had been, why I was feeling the ways I was feeling, and start implementing tools to begin to love myself through the struggles I had in the past and the struggles I had in that current moment. Looking at myself as a third person has allowed me to reflect on every opportunity and challenge that comes my way and ask myself, what would I say to my best friend or to my daughter in this situation, what would I advise them to do? I also give myself the space to ask myself if this situation is good for me or not, which has allowed me to set boundaries and only take on responsibilities that feel good for me and where I am going. Looking at myself as a third person has allowed me to truly embrace who I am and take care of myself in all moments of my life, because I am able to use the challenges of my past to reflect on my future.

The next time an opportunity or a challenge comes your way, take a moment and reflect and ask yourself what you might say to a friend who came to you for advice. Take a bird's-eye view of the situation and really take a moment to see what is happening and ask yourself if how you see yourself from a bird's-eye view is what you want in your life. If it is not, don't be afraid to say no, walk away and do what is best for you. Your future self will thank you for choosing you and for showing up for yourself. If a friend was in need, you would likely come running to be by their side and help them, so do the same for yourself and show up for yourself, pour into yourself, invest in yourself, give yourself what you need and make decisions that are going to add to your life. Show up for yourself and love yourself the same way you have consistently loved others. Give yourself the standing ovation that you have been giving others. I hope you can look at yourself as a third person, ask yourself if a situation is good for you and treat yourself the same way you would treat someone else in your life. I hope you can look at yourself as a third person and take your own advice. I hope you can look at yourself as a third person and love yourself the way you love others. I hope you can look at yourself as a third person and see how incredibly strong you are. Look at yourself as a third person and be compassionate and patient with yourself because you are doing the best you can. We deserve the same compassion that we give to others. You are not stuck in your pain. You are recovering, you are growing, and that is beautiful. I am cheering you on during your journey and I hope that, just like you may be cheering me or a friend on, you also choose to cheer yourself on.

Lesson Four

FROM MY MOM

"Don't Be Sorry, Be Conscious"

CHAPTER 4

GROWTH HAPPENS OUTSIDE OF YOUR COMFORT ZONES

Can you remember a time that you did something you knew your parents wouldn't like? Can you remember what it felt like to get punished or grounded for whatever you had done wrong? Can you remember how it felt when your parents were angry with you? I was just one of those kids who loved to push my parent's buttons and seemed to always be getting in trouble. Despite getting in trouble, I always wanted to be on my mom's good side. Any time I did something wrong as a child or teenager, I would write a full letter to her sharing how absolutely sorry I was for what I had done. Sometimes, I'd even cry a bit directly onto the letter, so she could see the wet marks to know I was so sorry that I was brought to tears. I really was just trying to trick her so I could get out of punishment sooner; sorry, Mom! My mom always accepted the apology, but she would always say to me, "Don't be sorry, be conscious." This lesson used to get under my skin as well. Not only did I have to spill my heart out in an apology, I also had to consciously think about what I did wrong so I didn't do it again in the future? It felt like torture! Looking back, however, I am grateful that she challenged me to critically think about what I had done wrong, so that I could reflect and ultimately grow to be the best version of me.

When you think about growth, you may think about challenging yourself to learn and do better, and that often comes with taking a step out of your comfort zone. Doing so requires you to consciously reflect on where you have been and where you want to be. Like many of us, you may have spent a good portion of your life inside of your comfort zone, afraid to step into an uncomfortable zone of risk taking and growth. It's okay if you feel stuck in your comfort zone and if you feel afraid of what is on the other side. As my mom would remind you, don't be sorry about all of the times in the past that you had chosen comfort over taking risks, but instead be conscious about it and ask yourself why you haven't taken those risks and what you need to do in order to feel secure in doing so.

To start that reflection, I encourage you to think back to when you were just a child, a child who was fearless and invincible and who thought that no goal or dream was out of reach.

I remember when I was a child, I was determined to be a singer, a firefighter, a hairdresser, and a doctor, all at the same time. At that time, nothing was going to stop me from living out these dreams. But then I grew up and society conditioned me to be afraid, to take only the calculated risks, the ones that make sense, the ones that aren't too daring or too bold, and the ones that guaranteed safety. Big dreams slipped away and smaller dreams took hold. I spent most of my adult life being afraid and not taking any risks, which led me to live a good portion of my life in regret. Although we all experience regret from time to time, my goal is that you don't have to feel stuck in your regret. I want you to take a moment here and reflect.

- Think back to when you were a child and ask yourself what your wildest dreams were.
- What are your dreams today?
- What can you not stop thinking about for your future?
- What step can you take today to get closer to reaching that goal?
- How can you challenge yourself to not be sorry about the past but to be conscious about steps you can take for your journey forward?
- What risk can you take in this moment, to change your life forever and reach the dream that your inner child wants for you?

Unfortunately, because our society has conditioned us to be afraid of going after our dreams, we stay in our comfort zone because it feels safer to do so. Instead, I encourage you to challenge what society has conditioned of you and choose to be bold, be courageous, be positive, and take the risk that has been tugging away at your heart. There is always a chance for "failure," but I believe that true failure does not exist, because if you "fail," you will learn lessons that you would not have learned had you stayed in your comfort zone. These lessons and new tools ultimately help you to grow. Yet, here again, it's not about feeling sorry for those times you have "failed" or made a mistake, it's about being conscious of what happened and realizing the life lessons you have just added to your toolkit that will only help you when you try again in the future.

All of the successful people and businesses started with just a dream, an idea, and a whole lot of hard work and passion. My college track coach used to tell us that we had to become comfortable with the uncomfortable. My race, in particular, was very uncomfortable. I ran the 400 meter dash and if you have ever ran it, you know exactly what I mean by how uncomfortable it is, especially at the end when the lactic acid builds in your legs and the true fatigue sets in. One of my mom's trademark cheers was to scream at every meet, "GOOO, IVY, PUSH, PUSH!" My mom cheered this exact cheer so often, that even my teammates can still visualize her saying it. It was yet another reminder from her to continue pushing, even when things got difficult or painful. This was her reminder that I had to step out of my comfort zones, push myself to take risks, and know that I had all I needed to reach my goals. The 400, along with many other obstacles in life, requires grit and perseverance to push through the uncomfortable, and even if it might feel impossible, it isn't. Allowing yourself to take a risk and become comfortable with the uncomfortable will allow you to thrive and reach levels in your life that you never thought were possible. If you always choose to stay comfortable and don't take risks that get you closer to your goals, you will never truly know what you have been capable of all along and you will never truly be able to reflect and be conscious of what you can do differently or more of in the future.

CHAPTER 4 | *LESSON FOUR*

What If I Don't Feel Ready?!

As you reflect on your goals, you may be feeling fear or anxiety because you do not feel quite ready to take that leap into the world of the unknown. You may not feel ready because you feel like you don't have all the answers or all the training or all the resources to accomplish your goal. The thing is, you may never feel *fully* ready, so why not just start? I have thought about writing this book for years. I had the idea in my head, I would get excited about it, and then fear kept me from putting pen to paper. I had fear about what people would think, fear about my ability to write a decent book, and fear that no one would even care or like what I had to say. I had so much fear that I never started. Until one day, I realized that I was never going to feel ready, but I knew deep in my heart that I wanted to write, to not only honor my mom, but to share the tools with you that I wish I had when I was younger and struggling with my mental health the most. One day, I just started writing, and here I am facing my fear, and here you are reading this book and showing that my fears were wrong all along. When I stepped out of my comfort zone, the flow of writing began, because I allowed myself to simply start, despite my fears. What if you played out in your mind what it would look like if you started taking steps toward your goals today and played out the exact scenario of everything going right? Visualizing your goals and visualizing everything working out as it should, can be just the push you need to start.

Sometimes it's about simply showing up and utilizing the tools and strengths you already have within you. Once you start, everything begins to fall into place and you learn that you never needed all of the education and resources upfront, all you needed was trust in yourself to just begin the journey and to take that leap of faith to get closer to the life you want and deserve. The most beautiful and magical moments happen when we decide we will no longer wait, but that we will decide to start now, trust the universe and know that everything will work out. You can choose to start, too, despite the fears, the naysayers, the limitations, you can start today and you can reach your goals. Your mind may tell you otherwise, but gently push out that negative thought and replace it with a positive one that if you just start and let things flow, no matter what happens, you can be proud of yourself that you chose to not let fear win. Don't limit yourself to the self-limiting beliefs you have had about yourself. You truly are capable of enduring and accomplishing the most difficult of tasks. You might not feel ready, but choose to start and do what scares you. You will likely surprise yourself along the way.

Stepping out of our comfort zones also means embracing change, which can be so hard for so many. Growing up, I hated change. My mom changed the layout of the furniture in our family room when I was a teenager, and I came home every day from school before she got home from work to change the furniture back to the way it was before it had been changed. She would then change the room back to how she wanted it, and we went back and forth like this for days until my mom got too tired of my desire for things to stay the same and kept the old arrangement. Even though change is scary, change is the one part of life that is always constant. People grow and move in and out of our lives, we change jobs or careers, we change our goals, we change styles, we change states, we change our eating habits, the list goes on and on. Despite the fear that change may bring, change also allows you to grow and forces you out of your comfort zone and into a zone of new beginnings. Without changing some parts of your life, you may never experience the beauty in new parts of your life that come from change. I am who I am because I have experienced changes in my life. And you are who you are because you have also experienced changes in your life. Even when the change coming in your life terrifies you, you can be conscious and reflect to find the positive in the change. If you are going through a change, even if you want to rearrange your furniture of your life back to how it was before when you were more comfortable with the couch on the right and the chair on the left, growth will come when you allow the room to change and turn into a new opportunity with a chance to flourish.

Whatever your goal is, even if it feels scary or far away, take that first uncomfortable step, because you never know where it will lead you. If you stay on the side of comfort, you may never experience the life changing moments of those uncomfortable experiences that not only get you closer to your goal, but mold you into a person that you have always wanted to be. To get something you've never had, you've got to do something you've never done. Every time we take a step outside of our comfort zones, we are proving to ourselves and the world that we are capable of a challenge, and we are allowing ourselves to embark on a journey of change and growth. And that is what self-love is all about, being able to love ourselves while still seeking self-growth and self-exploration. It's about forgiving yourself when you step out of comfort and mess up, and finding the inner strength to still celebrate yourself because you even took that step in the first place. Try your best to not just be sorry about the bumps of the past as you continue to grow, you can instead use that experience as a conscious reflection of what you do and don't want in your life and as motivation forward to take the risks that allow you to get closer to the life you deserve.

Our comfort zones are comfortable, but what would happen if you took that first conscious step into uncomfort? What if this experience outside of your comfort zone changes your life, and helps you to grow into a stronger and more resilient you? I truly believe that outside of our comfort zones is a beautiful journey of growth, and you are so deserving of that experience. Push yourself out of the boundaries and limits you have kept yourself behind. It's amazing how resilient and capable we truly are, if we just believe in ourselves. Choose to be conscious about what makes you feel comfortable and what makes you uncomfortable and choose to get comfortable with the uncomfortable. Choose to be conscious and reflect on what you want in your future, based on where you have been in your past and choose to do something that you have never done; you will end up with a wealth of new knowledge and discovery about yourself. Always remember to not be sorry about staying where you are, remain conscious about taking steps forward.

Lesson Five
FROM MY MOM

"It's Better To Be Pissed Off, Than To Be Pissed On"

CHAPTER 5

THERE IS STRENGTH IN FEELING YOUR FEELINGS - IT'S OKAY TO NOT BE OKAY

Have you ever had a really bad day where it feels like everything that can go wrong, goes wrong? I'm talking about those days when you slept past your alarm and missed an important meeting, said the wrong thing to someone, missed the bus, stubbed your toe, got your shirt stuck on a railing AND spilled your coffee all over yourself. Aren't those days just so frustrating? Have you ever been really, really angry with the world or with someone and just felt quite plainly, pissed off? If you've ever been pissed off before at someone or something, my mom would tell you that it's better to be pissed off, than to be pissed on. This was by far one of my mom's funniest sayings, but yet such a true and powerful reminder for us to know that it is okay to feel the way that we are feeling. She was letting us know that it was much better to be pissed off, than to have our dog or someone else use the bathroom on us! This statement is a funny yet powerful reminder that it is truly okay to not be okay. Unfortunately, in our society, we don't often hear from others that it is okay to not be okay, we instead hear things like, "Someone else has it worse than you, so it could be worse," or "It's really not that big of a deal; you are overreacting." Sound familiar at all? When we hear these messages, we in turn decide that we shouldn't talk about what we are going through, and that it feels safer to keep everything bottled up on the inside. These statements only invalidate how we are feeling and often lead us to not only struggle in silence, but also feel like we have to show the world that we are okay and happy, when on the inside we feel like we are falling apart. Struggling in silence is not only mentally exhausting, it can also prolong your mental health problems and make them worse, as they will go unaddressed. All of this may sound very, very familiar to you and if it does, it's not your fault that you feel this way. Unfortunately, the stigma around mental health has felt so big and so real for so many of us. There are so many of us walking around everyday upset, angry, pissed off, and afraid to talk about it, because we are afraid of being judged by others, afraid that our feelings will be unheard or misunderstood or invalidated, or afraid that we will be a burden on other people. You are not alone in these feelings, as I had experiences in my life where my struggles were invalidated and this only furthered my belief that not only was it easier, but it was also safer to struggle in silence.

Through writing this book, I've been reflecting a lot on the past. I can always count on Facebook to bring up memories of the past and these memories will either have me cringing at my thirteen year old self, or provide a space for deep reflection. Facebook reminded me of a post from 2013, after our first time going to DII nationals for the 4×400 relay in college. Before the race even began, we were completely doubtful of ourselves and we could see the doubt in each other's eyes. The end result was not favorable as we performed terribly. I had already been struggling with anxiety and depression, and this outcome only furthered the self-hate and negative self-talk I was experiencing. I posted on Facebook, and instead of writing about how I was actually feeling, I only focused on the positive of the situation, and wrote about how this experience was going to help teach us life lessons, and that we were only going to come back stronger. There is nothing wrong with having a positive perspective in a tough situation, it can actually be beneficial (more about that in chapter 8 where my mom's lesson is to keep positive). However, toxic positivity is when you are so positive about a situation, that you neglect to feel what you are feeling and brush those negative feelings off completely. As we've talked about, doing this only heightens that mental health problem you are experiencing and can lead you to struggle longer than if you had dealt with the problem in that moment. Instead, it's important to recognize how tough the situation might be and that it is okay to feel angry or sad or let down about it, and when you can validate your own feelings, that is when the true healing begins.

As I reflected on this Facebook post, I thought about the many other posts just like it, where I covered up the pain that I was actually feeling because I was unable to say "I'm not okay." It was easy to cover up the pain with a nice Facebook post, or with a smile and a laugh. I also reflected on how I would post on Facebook just to receive the validation I needed, and in the comments I saw multiple people saying how proud they were of me and my positive outlook on a bad situation. These comments provided the external validation of the self-worth I was looking for and only continued to validate my need to cover up what was really happening below the surface. I didn't talk about how yet another bad performance made me feel like a failure and how much the feelings I was having bothered me relentlessly for months. I didn't talk about how this experience only increased my feelings of self-hatred. I didn't talk about how that experience only led to increased anxiety and decreased performance toward reaching my goals. I read that post and I can reflect now on how much I've grown. I still struggle with my mental health, lack of self confidence, negative self-talk, anxiety, validation seeking, and grief, and that's okay, I spent many years of my life struggling, and many of those struggles can often resurface, just like they may for you. The difference for me now is that I am okay asking for help. The difference is I am okay with saying to someone that I am not okay. I can recognize the lesson in the situation, but I will also allow myself to feel. I can try my best to remain positive so that I can keep moving forward, but I can also recognize that positivity doesn't mean my other feelings are not valid. It isn't about reaching a destination of happiness, it's about loving yourself through the journey and knowing you are worthy of your tomorrow. You may struggle, but you are also strong, bold and beautiful. You can be all of those things at the same time. As you grow on this journey and allow yourself to open up and get real about your struggle, you will encounter even more people just like you, just trying to figure it all out, one day at a time.

    Just like Facebook allowed me to reflect, I ask that you reflect as well about where you are at right now. So often, we brush off our feelings as insignificant because we say that the situation isn't bad enough to warrant discussion or compassion, but what you are going through is important and valid. If you are having that really bad day and you are just pissed off, that is completely okay to have moments, days or weeks that are just really, really hard. No matter if you are upset or frustrated about a relationship, a test you didn't do well on, a conversation that did not go as you expected it to, or even a stubbed toe-if it's bothering you, it's bothering you and it matters simply because you matter as you are in this moment. The more that we brush our feelings off as insignificant, the larger those feelings will become and the longer our struggle will be. So I want you to ask yourself, what are you feeling at this very moment? What are you angry, confused, pissed off, upset or disappointed about? Even though it can be incredibly uncomfortable to sit with those feelings, I encourage you to sit in the sadness, or the anger, or the regret, and remind yourself that what you are going through is valid and important and that you are worthy of working through this situation. When you allow yourself to truly feel how you are feeling, you can then reflect on what you need to keep moving forward, whether that be reaching out for help from a friend or a therapist, or if it means practicing self-care and taking a walk to take a break and clear your mind. Taking that next step toward what you need to feel better, is when the true healing begins. This reflection will allow us to see that it's okay to be pissed off because we are worthy of feeling that feeling.

As we reflect on what it truly means to be okay with not being okay and to know that it's better to be pissed off than pissed on, it's also important to remember that our mental health journeys are not linear. Unfortunately, it is likely that you will experience stress and difficult times in the future; that is just part of life. We will have good days, where we will celebrate our accomplishments and have joy in our lives, and then we will have really tough days, where we will struggle and feel low. However, it is within those challenging days that we grow in strength and resiliency to get through difficult times in the future. Having tough times doesn't make you a failure, but instead actually teaches you what works for you, as your own unique individual. Without those tough times, we wouldn't know what works to help us feel grounded or what works to provide us with comfort and healing. So when you struggle in the future, ask yourself, what did you do before when you were struggling in the past that helped you then, and feel empowered to know that you can take the time to do that activity again to see if it helps this time. You aren't stuck, you have the tools within you to keep putting one foot in front of the other, and work through this challenging time.

Grant yourself that space to feel how you feel, let your emotions out in ways that feel good for you by giving yourself permission to cry, laugh, run, dance it out, scream, cry some more, talk to someone or find a quiet space for yourself. Give yourself permission to be who you are in this moment and every moment moving forward. Refuse to let the emotions you are feeling now dictate who you are and how far you have come. Know that you are not alone, we are all going through our own struggles, and no matter how big or how small they may seem to us or to others, it is important to know that it is okay to feel how you feel no matter how seemingly small the problem. Breathe and have faith that you will be granted another day to wake up and look in the mirror and realize how magnificently beautiful you are, despite the pain. Today, whatever you are going through, embrace your unique journey and remember to love yourself through it. You may make mistakes, you may have setbacks, you may endure many defeats, but you will be a stronger person because of it. You will love yourself more for being genuinely honest with yourself in this growing and healing process. You will fall seven times and pick yourself up eight. You will keep fighting for you, because you are worth fighting for.

Despite Being Pissed Off, You Can Get Those Feelings Off Your Chest And Talk About Them - It's Better Than Being Pissed On!

As we are reminded by my mom that it's better to be pissed off than to be pissed on, we've talked a lot about how it's okay to be pissed off and feel your feelings, but we also need to address that it's okay to talk about those feelings. I know firsthand how hard and frightening it can be to reach out for help and tell someone how you are feeling. I will forever be grateful for a friend of mine, who over a casual lunchtime date, told me that she was struggling with her mental health, and that she was getting help for her struggle through therapy. This was the most pivotal step for me in my healing journey, to hear from a friend who also looked like she had it all together, that she was struggling and doing something about that struggle. That was the first time the stigma I believed around mental health began to break down, and truly empowered me to get the help I had so desperately needed my entire life. The first person I wanted to call about my decision to start therapy was my mom. My mom always knew on the surface that I was stressed out, but she never realized how much my anxiety was affecting me in every area of my life, because I never talked about it. Making the call to my mom filled me with fear, but her patience and acceptance on the other side of the phone gave me comfort that I was making the right decision. Making a conscious decision to open up every week to a therapist about what I was going through was foreign and uncomfortable. I went from hiding behind my smile and struggling in silence, to having to share the ins and outs of my feelings with someone. But therapy healed me, saved my life, and gave me tools to work through challenges which ultimately gave me hope for my future. Therapy allowed me to see that society has it all wrong when we are told that talking about what we are going through is a sign of weakness. Using your voice and reaching out for help is the strongest thing you can ever do, because you've recognized that you want more for yourself and you realized that you can't do that alone, and that is more than okay.

I like to think about seeking help, whether it be from a friend, teammate, coach, teacher, parent, partner, or a professional like a therapist, as removing layers of a mask. The mask is one that we hide behind that shows the world we are okay when we are not. The mask leads us to struggle in silence and is a comfortable and safe mask. Removing a layer of that mask can feel overwhelming. There's a lot of fear behind removing a layer of the mask and exposing what's really behind that outer layer of "being okay," especially because you are not sure how it is going to be received by someone. You might also not know who to even start with to reach out about your problems because you feel that you are alone. But I can promise you that you are not alone, even when your mind tries to tell you that you are. There is always someone in your corner who wants to help you through what you are going through and try their best to understand your unique situation. Unfortunately, because of the stigma, we might not always receive the responses that we want when we open up, and that can be really hard to digest, especially after you have built up the courage to even talk to somebody. But there are many people in this world who love you and who want to help you, so I encourage

CHAPTER 5 | *LESSON FIVE*

and challenge you to not give up hope, and to try again and talk to somebody else, because there is *always* someone else who wants to help.

At the end of this book, in the appendix, you will find a list of online resources that you may want to take advantage of, as it may feel easier to start using your voice and reach out for help with someone you don't know but who is trained to help you through your situation. The resources in the appendix will also assist you in finding a therapist in your area. When finding a therapist, it can feel a lot like dating, you may have to try a few therapists out, until you find the right fit for you. If you don't like your therapist, it may feel that therapy isn't beneficial for you, but that may not be the case, it might be that you need to find another therapist who fits better with your unique personality and your unique needs, and that is more than okay. Know that you have your family, friends, colleagues, teammates, strangers, and even myself, to help you in this current challenge and any future challenge.

I encourage you to remove a layer of your mask and start at the most surface level issue. This may look like just telling someone that you are struggling with getting tasks done. Maybe beneath that issue, there are a lot of problems surrounding lack of self-worth or confidence, or anxiety, or even depression, but start with that surface level issue, because that might feel big enough to share. Being vulnerable is scary and tough work, so when you are ready to open up about even that surface level issue, give yourself some credit and celebrate that you just accomplished something huge for yourself and your mental wellness. When you share that surface level issue and you realize how good it feels to get the weight of that problem off your chest and feel heard by someone then it gets a little bit easier each time to share the deeper problems and have someone by your side to work through those problems. Once you take that first step, you embark on a journey to keep walking forward, steadfast in your ability to open up a little bit more with each step. Until one day, you can tell someone you are not fine, rather than covering it up for days, months or longer. By opening up about how you are truly feeling, you allow yourself to begin healing. Once you begin healing, that's when you learn those life lessons; that's when you are able to reflect and grow and look back and say to yourself, "Wow, I used to think the safest place was living behind the lie that I was okay, but I realized the safest and best place to grow is to live closest to my truest self and not deny my feelings."

Reflect on who is in your support system and what resources are available to you to reach out and talk about your pain. Remember that your pain is valid, and that by talking about it, you can begin to set yourself free and release yourself of some of that pain. By talking about it, you unleash the weight of it, but you also identify tools to help you keep moving forward. Remember that your smile is beautiful, but you don't have to hide behind it. You can show that behind your smile is a story full of good and bad, a story of growth, a story that is yours, a story of resilience, a story of pushing forward, finding your voice, reaching out for help, learning your power, and giving yourself grace to start again.

Feel your feelings–the good, the bad, the sad, the frustrating, the uncomfortable, the disappointing, the anxiety provoking moments, the depression, the relationship struggles or the feeling of being overwhelmed. Feel all of it. You can break free from society's restrictions that tell you you need to be okay and happy all of the time, because it is truly okay if you aren't. It is always okay to not be okay. Give yourself grace on your hard days and know that what you are going through is valid. You are not a failure because you have struggled, you are thriving and growing. Struggling makes us who we are, imperfectly beautiful. Feeling your feelings and reflecting on how you are doing is the first step in healing to ask yourself what you need to work through this struggle. So be pissed off, really feel how pissed off you are, it's okay, because remember, at least you aren't being pissed on!

Lesson Six
FROM MY MOM (PART 1)

"Take Care Of Those Teeth!"

CHAPTER 6

YOU ARE MORE THAN YOUR TO-DO LIST - HOW TO TAKE CARE OF YOUR MENTAL HEALTH

This chapter on self-care is so important that you get two lessons from my mom! We'll start with another one that I heard quite often growing up, "Take care of those teeth!" My mom and her family grew up very poor and they did not have knowledge or finances to see the dentist. Because of this, my mom had several dental issues in her adult life that cost her time, energy and money. She didn't want my brother and I to struggle like she did, and so she stayed on top of us to make sure that we always took care of our teeth. To this day, I strive to do the best I can with brushing, flossing, and seeing the dentist twice a year. I have always done a great job taking care of my teeth as well as my physical health, but it never came quite as easily for me to take care of my mental health. You may feel the same, where you find it easier to take care of your physical health than your mental health. Our physical health includes taking care of the pieces of ourselves that people can see, and so often we have an easier time taking care of ourselves physically because there is an expectation to. This lesson, however, should be a reminder for us all that just like we are often encouraged to take care of our physical health, we also have to take care of our mental health.

Our minds and our bodies are interconnected. Growing up, I always had constant headaches and stomachaches and I spent hours in the doctor's office trying to figure out what was going on with me physically. After countless tests, the doctors were unable to find anything truly wrong with me in a physical sense. I now realize that these physical pains were my body's way of telling me that I was struggling mentally. You may have experienced this in your life as well. Think back to a presentation you had to make in class that you were incredibly anxious for–you may remember your heart racing, your hands sweating, your stomach turning, your head pounding, or you may even remember not being able to keep any food down because you were just too nauseous from the nerves. Your physical body was affected by the anxiety you were experiencing! On the other hand, if you are an athlete or enjoy working out and then you experience an injury, you may feel frustrated, disappointed or struggle with depression as you are unable to workout or compete in your sport alongside your teammates. Our physical abilities or lack of physical abilities can also impact our mindset.

The same thought can be applied to our teeth. If you have had problems with your teeth, you may struggle with self-confidence around smiling and that can impact your overall well being. And if you are struggling with your mental health, you may have a hard time finding the energy to even brush your teeth, because when we are struggling so deeply, it can feel almost impossible to find the energy to do daily tasks. If you do not take care of your teeth, the problems you will experience when you visit the dentist will only continue to pile up. The same applies to our mental health, if we don't take the time to really allow ourselves to feel and work through a bad day, it can turn into a series of bad days that can lead to larger mental health problems, such as overwhelming anxiety or depression. The more we regard our physical or mental health problems as insignificant, the larger those problems grow. And if we are unable to seek out help or practice self-care, then we may not feel able to take care of ourselves physically, we may stop taking care of our teeth, or stop getting physical exercise, or stop eating the right foods. Therefore your mental health issues can also impact your physical health, which in turn shows how important it is to take care of both our physical health and our mental health, because they are both so intertwined.

When you are feeling really stressed or overwhelmed, where does it show up in your body? Does your jaw clench up? Do you grind your teeth? Do you get instant headaches or stomach aches? Do your shoulders tense up? Take a moment and think about where stress shows up for you in your own body as a way to see how linked your mind and body are. I want you to ask yourself how you can ensure you are taking care of your mind, just like you may take care of your body. Our mental health is easier for ourselves and others to ignore, because we cannot see it like we do when someone has a broken leg or cold symptoms. We are quick to go to the gym or join a running club to run a marathon to meet our physical health goals, but we find it harder to talk to a friend, find a therapist or practice self-care for our mental health goals. In order to work through the pain you may be experiencing, you have to take that first scary but important step in taking care of your mental health, whatever that might mean for you. Just like I was reminded to take care of my teeth after almost every disappointing dentist appointment my mom had, I am reminding you to take care of your mental health. Because there is only one you, and your mind deserves the same treatment you give to your body, your mind deserves to be shown up for in the same capacity.

I challenge you to find time each day to do something for you and your mental health. It is easy to get angry with ourselves when we don't accomplish all that we want to in the short and sweet twenty-four hours of each day. However, we do have a choice to be kind to ourselves during those hours. Some days we may have a goal to get ten tasks done, but it is okay if you can realistically only do three or four of those tasks, or if you can even only do one of those tasks. It's okay if you don't get to everything on your list. I want you to trust the process and to remind yourself that although you might not get everything done in this moment, things can and will get done, exactly when they need to be done. It's important during the chaos of your day to take breaks that will allow you to be more effective at the task at hand and allow you to refresh your mind. Forgive yourself when you slept in a little too late, or accidentally fell asleep early when you wanted to get work done. I promise you that work is still going to be there, but what matters most is your sense of mental wellness. We all have the same twenty-four hours and society pressures us to utilize those hours wisely otherwise we may be deemed as lazy or a failure. But I say we celebrate being okay if our twenty-four hours didn't go as planned and know that above all else on our lengthy to-do lists, our mental health should come first. You are more than everything on your to-do list, take care of you first. The work and chores will always be there, so find time to take care of yourself first, which will allow you to be your best whole self, mind, body, and soul in every situation you encounter.

Lesson Six
FROM MY MOM (PART 2)

"Don't Be A Superhero"

CHAPTER 6 | *LESSON SIX (PART 2)*

Superheroes are often the ones to save the day and to pick up all of the puzzle pieces and put them back together. My mom would remind me that I didn't always have to be a superhero and that I didn't and shouldn't have to do it all. I didn't have to do it all when it came to chores in the house, or work for a group project, or taking care of others. When we are superheroes for everyone else, we forget about ourselves. You can be a superhero for others, but at what cost? If you're always the one doing everything for others, people may stop doing those same things for themselves and expect you to always pick up the slack. In the process, you not only lose time for yourself, you build resentment for others as they take a back seat in helping you out.

In addition to wanting to be everything for everyone, society will often encourage you to be part of every personal and professional opportunity that comes your way, even if it adds more stress to your plate. It's often really hard to say no to these opportunities. Saying no and setting boundaries means realizing that we actually can't do everything, and that reality can be really hard to digest. Saying no means that we might miss out on an opportunity that could change our lives forever. Saying no may also cause fear that we will be less liked by others, when so many of us are wanting to be superheroes so that everyone will like us. But what does saying yes get for us, when we already have too much on our plates? Saying yes causes more anxiety, stress, anger, and fear about how you will get everything done. Saying yes may make more people like us, but we may lose ourselves and our own sense of self-love in the process. We all have the same twenty-four hours, and there is only so much that can get done in that time frame before you begin to lose your sense of self. Saying yes when you are already overwhelmed shouldn't be something that is admired or desired. Instead, it should be admired by society to say no to opportunities when you are overwhelmed. Saying no is a beautiful form of self-care because when we say no, we make a conscious decision to look after ourselves and put ourselves and our mental wellness first. By saying no, you can take care of yourself and create space for mental wellbeing, which is a beautiful gift that you can give to yourself to benefit you in the long term. Saying no is a way to realize that not everyone is going to like you, even if you say yes to every opportunity, and that's okay, because saying no is a way of finding your worth. No matter what you do, there will always be someone who doesn't like you. Just like you don't like every single person that you meet, not everyone will like you, and that is okay, even when it's hard to digest. It can be difficult if you have spent your entire life saying yes, for fear of letting others down, for fear of not being liked, or for fear of letting yourself down for not being able to "do it all." But by saying no, you give yourself permission to have the necessary space and time for you to care about yourself and grow. If the opportunity will help you to grow and make you happy, and add to your self-care rather than add stress, then it is absolutely okay to say yes to it. But if the opportunity or relationship will be a detriment to your mental health, self-worth and self care, know that you have the strength to say no. You can say yes to opportunities when they feel good, and say no when you know the best choice will be focusing on the responsibilities you already have, with the most important one of focusing on you.

CHAPTER 6 | *LESSON SIX (PART 2)*

Saying no can be hard to do, but it is also really liberating. I am a true believer that things come to us for a reason, and they leave us for a reason. Saying no to an opportunity that isn't good for you, or that will take up too much of your mental space, doesn't mean you will never see that opportunity again, it means that an even better opportunity is coming. The universe will thank you for taking care of you and for making a decision that puts you first, and the universe will come back full circle with more opportunities, more relationships, and more avenues for success. You owe it to yourself to put yourself first and recognize that if you need more time for yourself, you can take that time and are worthy of that time.

I hope you can be a superhero for yourself for a change and choose to say no to opportunities that are not good for you and say yes to investing in yourself. I hope you can be a superhero for yourself and ask yourself what you need in this very moment to get through the challenge you may be facing. I hope you can be a superhero for yourself and choose you, knowing that you matter as you are and you deserve to take care of your mental health. My mom would want you to remember that you don't have to be a superhero for everyone else and you don't have to be everything for everyone. You can only do so much, and when you do too much, you lose focus of what is most important to you, and you lose focus on taking care of yourself.

How can we actually put these lessons from my mom around taking care of ourselves mentally and physically and setting boundaries into practice? Here are some key reminders for self-care, as well as some hands-on tools you can use!

Know That Self-Care Won't Be An Overnight Fix For Your Problem

We often seek something that's going to make us feel 100 percent better when we are not feeling good, physically or mentally. We are often looking for a quick and complete fix, but more often than not, healing takes time. After a surgery from a broken bone, the doctors will give you medication and advise you to rest, both of which will eventually make you feel better, but you won't be back at your 100 percent for some time. This process of healing is the same for our mental health, we have to be patient with our minds like we are with our bodies. Self-care, therapy and medication for our mental health are not overnight fixes, and will take time for you to get to where you want to be mentally. Self-care does not always fully fix your problem. Let's say you have an opportunity where you have to somehow find the courage to turn down, and that is causing you a lot of stress and let's say your self-care jam is taking a walk and being outside in nature. If you go out and take that walk, that tough conversation to turn down that opportunity, also known as the "problem," still exists, but taking that walk outside can give you the grace and space to feel even just a little bit better and to move through the problem easier with more clarity on how exactly you will turn the opportunity down, or how you will calm your mind before the conversation. Instead of seeking out a self-care technique that makes you feel 100 percent better, look for something that makes you feel 25 percent better, or even just 5 percent better. Taking time for self-care that helps you to feel even just a little bit better can be the push you need to continue moving forward through the issue you are having.

For me, exercise has always been my saving grace for my mental health when I am struggling. Exercise never takes away the problem I am facing, but it makes me feel a lot, or even just a little bit, better than I did before. And by feeling just a little bit better, I give myself permission to provide myself with grace and compassion for the rest of the day, just by doing something for me. Mental health and recovery are a journey and your journey will be a unique one, different from my own and different from those around you. I am often asked how long it took me to start feeling better. Although I can roughly answer that question for you, I do not want you to have an expectation of how long it will take for you to feel better. You are your own unique person with your own unique struggle, so be patient with yourself as you work through your own journey. The key to this journey of ups and downs is compassion, patience, self-love and ultimately knowing that even if what you did today only made you feel a little bit better, that is enough. Keep going. Don't get down on yourself if you are not back at your own version of 100 percent yet, take things one step at a time. You are healing and learning what works for you on this journey, and that is beautiful.

Find What Works For You

Find YOUR self-care jam. I am going to share with you a few self-care techniques, but you have to find what tool works best for you. You are a unique individual and you might not be someone who does well with meditation, but thrives with exercise–that's okay to stick with what feels good for you. Also remember that self-care changes with time and what may have worked for you in the past, may no longer work as effectively. You are not a failure if you need additional self-care in your day to work through this new challenge you are experiencing. You are constantly growing and changing, let your self-care grow and change with you.

Try different self-care tools until you find ones that work best for you. Write down the self-care tools you enjoy to add to your "self-care toolkit" and know you can pull these tools out in times of anxiety, stress, overwhelm or sadness.

A few ideas include:

- **Letting Out Your Feelings**: Talking to a friend, parent, coach, or a therapist. We learned that, "It's better to be pissed off than pissed on," so use your voice and know that you are able and worthy to reach out for help. You can also journal or draw out your feelings as well. Expressing your feelings in a way that feels good for you is a way to unpack the heaviness of that feeling, and often that can be healing and rejuvenating.
- **Moving Your Body:** You can move your body anywhere, anytime as a way to practice self-care. Are you feeling overwhelmed while reading as you reflect on your journey? Are you feeling stressed as you walk to an office to have a tough conversation? Take a moment and put this book down and stretch your arms way above your head, move them across your chest, and reach down for your toes. Simply stretching can be so helpful. Remember the body and mind are so interconnected, take advantage of moving your body for your mental health. Movement sends messages to your brain that help to reduce stress

and anxiety. You can also move by going for a walk or a run, exercising, or doing yoga.

- **Take A Break And Do Something You Enjoy:** Take a break from your busy lifestyle and do something that brings you joy. Watch a funny movie, play video games, dance in your room, listen to music to help give you a good cry or music that helps pump you up; whatever it is, take that break. Your mind and body will thank you for taking a break from all that is on your to-do list and taking that break will allow you to be that much more effective at the activities you were doing before, because you've allowed yourself to reset. Remember, your mental health and self-care are the most important tasks on that to-do list.

- **Meditation/Finding Mindful Moments:** The beauty of meditation is that you have your breath at any time as a tool to use to calm your mind in a stressful situation. A few deep breaths can be incredibly healing. I challenge you to just take two deep breaths right now and feel the calming energy those breaths create. You can also meditate by finding mindful moments within your day. During your next shower, you can allow yourself to feel the calming nature of the warm water, rather than thinking about all you have to do later that day. During your next walk, instead of checking social media and texting friends, you can focus on your feet planted on the ground and the fresh air on your body. These are ways to be mindful during your day and allow yourself to mentally reset. Mindfulness allows you to see that you may not be able to change the past, and you cannot control what will happen in the future, but you can be here in this current moment and that can allow peace and calm to enter your world. You can practice mindfulness, anywhere, at any time. Mindfulness is a powerful example of how self-care does not have to be expensive or lengthy to be effective.

- **Positive Affirmations/Gratitude:** Write down five positive affirmations about yourself and five things you are grateful for in your life and make this a consistent practice in your day. Practicing positivity for yourself and gratitude for the people and things in your life can reduce negative emotions and promote overall wellbeing and happiness. The more you write those positive affirmations, the more you believe them, the more your body embodies them!

Which of these self-care tools will you try for yourself? What other self-care tools work for you? Self-care doesn't have to feel like a chore, find something that you enjoy and utilize that tool whenever you are having a challenging time.

Manage Pain With Joy

I found out that I was pregnant one week before my mom passed away, so throughout my entire pregnancy, I was learning how to manage the grief of losing my best friend with the joy of gaining the sweetest baby. I had to realize that it was okay to feel joyful, despite the grief, and finding those moments of joy have been what keep me going. I often feel both joy and grief on a daily basis and sometimes one overpowers the other. I'm learning more and more that that's okay.

Even if you are struggling right now with pain or grief in one area of your life, you are still allowed to feel joy or excitement in other parts of your life. By finding joy and light in each day, healing comes easier. I challenge and encourage you to do something that adds light to your life, despite the sadness you may feel. This will truly allow you to take time to feel the feeling you are having, but then ask yourself what you need and what you can do to feel a little bit better, or what you can do to add light to your day or to the moment. It's not about thinking that your pain isn't valid or important, it's acknowledging that you have pain, but you are still worthy of feeling joy.

At the end of each day, ask yourself what the highlight of your day was. I have made that a consistent practice in my household with my daughter. Challenge yourself even on the hardest of days to find the light within the darkness–because the light is there, even when it doesn't feel like it, the light is there, guiding you through the darkness to truly experience the joy on the other side of the pain. Wherever you are in your journey, I encourage you to find the light today and know that I am proud of you, and I hope one day, you feel proud of you, too.

Self-Care Is Going To Look Different At Different Times In Your Life

As you venture through your mental wellness journey, you may find that you need more self-care in certain situations or that the self-care techniques that worked for you a few months ago are no longer as effective. You may have been finding a lot of benefit from ten minute meditations each morning, but then you are hit with stressful news about someone important in your life, and it may feel like that ten minute meditation is not giving you the same benefit it used to. It's okay to either try to do a longer meditation, add in another self-care technique throughout your day such as journaling, seek out an additional therapy session, or try a whole new self-care technique that you have never tried before. Just like when we are working out and only use ten-pound dumbbells for each exercise, our bodies eventually get used to that particular weight and our progress may slow down. It can be helpful to switch up our self-care techniques when our bodies get "used" to them. You may always benefit from the same self-care technique and never need to change it up, but you also may need a change, and it is more than okay to try a new self-care technique or add additional self-care to your day, especially when you are experiencing a new challenge.

Always remember to take care of your mental health the same way you take care of your teeth and your physical health, and remember that the best kind of superhero is one that shows up for themselves, too.

Lesson Seven

FROM MY MOM

"Organization Is the Key To Life"

CHAPTER 7

CREATING A SELF-CARE ROUTINE

My brother and I hated cleaning our rooms, but it always felt like we were being told that our rooms needed to be clean before we could do anything fun. My mom constantly reminded us that we needed to keep our rooms not only clean, but organized and she would say to us, despite our moans and groans, that "organization is the key to life." My mom was big on organization. It's been fairly easy for us since her passing to go back and look at old photo albums because she made sure they were all organized very well. She taught us to be organized and encouraged us to write the dates on everything, so we could keep track in the future. As I have my own house now with multiple rooms, I am realizing that she was truly right about this lesson and that it is so much easier to find items if they are organized. I am truly grateful for this lesson she taught me.

When the spaces that you live and work in are organized, you are able to find things that you need more easily and often a clutter free space can lead to a clutter free mind. While you work on organizing the spaces that you live in, it is important to think about how you will organize your self-care into your day to day life. As you figure out what self-care tools work best for you and recognize that self-care may change with different circumstances, or that you might need more self-care in tough situations, it's also important for you to find small moments throughout your day to continuously practice self-care. So many of us choose to wait until our mental or physical health gets "bad enough" to begin taking care of ourselves. If we wait until things get really bad, our healing journey will be prolonged and the issues will be larger, rather than if we'd dealt with the issue upfront. If you're having a bad day or if you are stressed about all that you need to get done, you can practice self-care. I challenge you to find time every day to do something for you, something that makes you feel good and something that helps you to reset.

How Can You Make Organization Around Your Self-Care The Key To Your Life And Build A Self-Care Routine?

Be Intentional About Your Self-Care

Check in with yourself at least twice a day and ask yourself how you are feeling at that moment. Ask yourself how you are feeling from 0 to 100 percent and know that not every day will be at 100 percent or even at 50 percent and that is more than okay. You can have good and bad moments within one day, so it's important to check in with yourself often to see how you are feeling. When you check in with yourself, you give yourself permission to ask what you need to feel better or who you can reach out to for help. By doing this, you choose to acknowledge that your feelings are

CHAPTER 7 | *LESSON SEVEN*

significant and give yourself the self-care tools you need to know you are worth fighting for.

Build Time For Mindful Moments Within Your Day

You may be reading and thinking that you have no time to practice self-care. I will stop you there–you are actually making the time right now. You are reading these pages and doing something right now for your mental health by challenging the negative thoughts in your mind and empowering yourself to take the next step in your mental wellness journey. Celebrate yourself for that!

Taking advantage of the tasks that you already do every day and implementing mindfulness into those moments is a powerful way to see that you don't need a ton of extra time to practice self-care. Every day you likely take a shower, brush your teeth or eat a meal. During these daily tasks, we often are texting, thinking about the next part of our day, or just generally feeling anxious. The next time you brush your teeth, say three positive affirmations to yourself while you are otherwise mindlessly brushing. The next time you eat a meal, put your phone down, truly taste the food you are eating, be in this current moment. Feel the water running down your body during your next shower, or your feet planted on the ground on your next walk around the house or outside–these are ways to build mindfulness into your daily life. You can also write down positive quotes and post them around your room or have them on your phone to refer back to when you are feeling down. This can be a simple, yet effective way to build positivity into your day.

Set Reminders to Practice Self-Care

Set reminders on your phone or on sticky notes around your room to remind yourself to practice self-care. Be specific about those reminders and include what self-care technique you will be practicing. My phone every morning reminds me to "practice self-love affirmations" and for me that is my signal to pull out my journal and write down my affirmations and gratitude statements.

Practice Self-Care At A Time When It Feels Good For You

If you are not a morning person, you don't have to force yourself to wake up five minutes early to start your self-care routine. Instead, maybe you feel most productive and energized in the afternoon or the evenings, you can take advantage of those times of day to practice your self-care. When you make the intention to practice self-care at the times of the day when you are naturally the most motivated, you will be more inclined to actually practice self-care.

Organize Your Self-Care Tools And Write Them Down

Actually take a moment and write down all of your self-care tools. Write down what makes you feel calm when you are stressed out, what makes you feel joy when you are sad, what makes you feel at peace when you are frustrated. You may have a different self-care technique for each of these emotions. Maybe when you are stressed out, meditation calms you down, but when you are feeling really sad and disappointed, watching funny movies or talking to a trusted friend cheers you up and keeps you grounded. Write down your self-care tools and when you can use each of those tools. Writing them down provides your mind with a safe place to land when you are feeling overwhelmed. If you're like me, when you are overwhelmed, your mind tells you that nothing is going to help you feel any better. When you have your self-care tools written down, you can refer back to them and remind yourself that there *are* tools you can use to work through this challenging situation.

Have An Accountability Partner

You are never alone in what you are going through. I can guarantee that there is someone in your circle of friends or family who is struggling with something right now at this moment. There is likely someone else also looking for ways to take care of themselves but is unsure how to start or how to stay consistent. Having someone in your life such as a friend, partner, coach or parent that you can reach out to as an accountability partner can be key to staying organized and consistent with your self-care routine. Find a person who you can share your self-care tools with so that when you forget what works for you, they can remind you of your tools, and even practice them with you. It may be helpful for you to have someone check in about how you are sticking to your self-care goals, not for judgment but for support. It can be helpful as well to practice self-care with someone in your life who is also struggling or who is also looking to stick to a self-care routine. You and your accountability partner can go on walks together, check in with each other, meditate together, journal together, or do any other self-care technique together. Sometimes our mental health journeys can feel isolated and lonely, but you are never alone. Utilize the support people you have in your network and ask someone in your life to help you stick to your self-care goals and to practice self-care with you.

Be Patient With Yourself If You "Fall Back" On Your Routine

I know I have experienced times in my life where I was not as good about practicing self-care as I should have been. It's so easy to feel frustrated with ourselves in those moments, or to feel like we have taken ten steps backwards. You are not a failure if you have a lapse in time where you didn't practice self-care. Self-love is a form of self-care and self-love is about having compassion, grace and patience toward ourselves. One of the strongest things you can do in life is say, "Today may not have been my best day, but I can try again tomorrow, and I am worthy of trying again tomorrow." Remember that the past does not dictate the future, and the past does not dictate your worth. You can start again, over and over and over. Just like when you clean your room, it gets messy again because you are living in it, and you have to continuously start the process of cleaning it up again and again.

Our self-care toolkits may need some organizing, but that's okay, it doesn't make you a failure if you need to organize your self-care or clean it up a bit. My mom would say that organizing your self-care toolkit makes you strong, because after all, organization is the key to life.

Lesson Eight
FROM MY MOM

"Keep Positive"

CHAPTER 8

FINDING LIGHT WITHIN THE DARKNESS AND KEEPING HOPE ALIVE

I can scroll through old texts with my mom and so many of them are reminders from my mom to "keep positive." My mom embodied positivity, particularly when she received her cancer diagnosis and throughout her fight against cancer. It did not matter what unfortunate news we received from the doctors, my mom always found a way to digest the information, cry about it, and then go right back to enjoying the life that was in front of her. This was such a beautiful way to view life. My mom was just someone who loved life and loved finding the joy in everything, even in the sad moments. Many people, including myself, admired her for how positive she was throughout her cancer journey. On social media, I shared a lot about the good and bad news we received during her fight with cancer and it was remarkable the amount of people who reached out to me and said that because of my mom and her positivity and upbeat personality, they felt empowered to stay positive during their own battle with cancer. My mom didn't realize how much she was empowering others, but she was. I truly believe she lived as long as she did with pancreatic cancer because she made a conscious choice to be positive as much as she could.

I remember during one of her chemo sessions, she told me a story about a colleague she had decades ago that was diagnosed with cancer. Everyone at the office felt so awful for him after hearing this unfortunate news, and they quickly began to worry about his chances of living much longer. A few short days later, an unfortunate random accident happened where the man was sitting in his car, and a truck fell onto his car, ending his life. I share this story because my mom would always say to me after we heard some tough news about her cancer that, "the truck hasn't fallen yet." The truck was her reminder to live life to the fullest, and that she very well may die from cancer, but she could also die from anything at any time. I strive to live my life in the way that she did, full of hope, love, and happiness. I hope you can see that you, too, have the option to keep positivity in your life. Although you can strive for positivity, you also want to make sure you are not experiencing toxic positivity, where you choose to be so positive all of the time, that you ignore any negative feeling you might be having. With toxic positivity, you might hear or think to yourself things like, "Just don't think about it, be positive" or "It could be worse" or "Positive vibes only!" What these statements do is take away the validity of what you are feeling. Instead, I want to remind you that what you are going through may be really hard and your feelings around this hard time are valid and important. Instead of toxic positivity, you can say things like, "I am really overwhelmed right now, but I am still worthy of love and acceptance and I am still worthy of having positive opportunities come my way." You don't have to feel positive or happy right now, but keeping positive is about remembering that you don't always have to feel this way, that there is light within the darkness, and that keeping hope alive can be beneficial for you as you navigate this journey.

If you aren't feeling positive right now, I see you and I understand. I spent most of my life thinking negative thoughts about the world around me and about myself. When I finally began my mental health and wellness journey, I also began my self-love journey. My self-love journey taught me the importance of being kind to myself during hard times, but also how to find moments of joy and light in those hard times. This has been a continuous journey for me throughout my life. When I lost my mom, I truly lost my sense of joy, but over time, I have been able to truly feel joy again. I can't help but smile when I think of how proud my mom would be of me right now for finding a newfound sense of happiness and keeping positive.

Even if you have lost your joy or sense of positivity, you can find it again and things can get easier in time. Your life can get brighter and feel brighter again. In spite of all the pain, it's important to hold onto hope, or at least lean into hope. Even just the smallest amount of hope can keep us moving forward. Keep hope alive that better days are coming. You aren't stuck, even if it feels that way; you have conquered tough times before and you will do it again. You are a warrior. It's okay if you're struggling and the joy in your life feels like it's been taken from you. I promise you, the joy is still there. With some work and patience, joy can surround you again. I hope you know that you can find those moments of joy, and even if they only make you feel good for a moment or two; those small moments add up and make a difference in your life.

What is your light within the darkness today? What is one positive part about today that you can hold onto as hope for tomorrow? Write down that one positive from the day, even if today feels dark and heavy, as a way to keep positivity in your life. I encourage you to sit with your feelings, reflect, ask yourself what you need, practice your self-care, and then challenge yourself to find something positive or hopeful to hold onto and carry you through. I encourage you to celebrate and enjoy this moment. The future is never promised, so rather than seeking out happiness in a destination, I hope you can find joy, love and gratitude in the now.

Taking the step into a world where you can seek out the positives can have a great impact on your overall mental health. Saying positive statements to yourself can help to improve your overall mood, sense of happiness and well-being. Although you may have spent your entire life being negative with yourself, it is never too late to implement positivity into your daily life. When you say positive statements to yourself, they may at first feel silly or superficial, they did for me. Change will not happen overnight, but consistent practice of positive statements and affirmations send positive messages to your brain, which your body begins to embody. What you say after "I am," is truly what you become. Unfortunately, we are often wired to think negative statements such as, "I am a failure" or "I am not good enough," and when we do that, we send a message to our brain to begin shutting us off from the opportunity before we even start.

I remember in college during my track career, I would get into the blocks before a race and immediately think, "I am not good enough to win this race." Despite all of the hard work I had been putting in at practice that should have proved to me that I was good enough, this negative statement sent a negative message to my brain, and I in turn did not run as well as I could have. Despite these negative thoughts, I still had a great track career, but unfortunately, due to the negative mindset that I had, it held me back from reaching my true potential and my true goals and in turn only created a journey of struggling with self-hate. My journey could have been a lot different if I had known the power of positivity back then. We act consistent with who we think we are, so if we think we are not good enough, we will then act not good enough and hold ourselves back from reaching our goals.

You may be thinking that just saying affirmations is not going to change your life or make a difference. You may be thinking, "I can't just tell myself that I am capable of lifting a 100 pound dumbbell when I know I can only lift thirty pounds." That may be true as we all do have limitations, but often it is not the limitation itself that holds us back, it is our mindset around those limitations that hold us back. The important part to hold onto is that having a positive mindset means you go to the gym prepared to get as safely close to 100 pounds as possible, which means that you are going to challenge yourself that for your squats today, you are going to pick up thirty-five pound dumbbells, instead of your usual thirty pounds. Maybe you even push yourself a little further and go for forty pounds, but maybe that is too heavy and you aren't able to finish the set, but you believed in yourself enough to try. In this scenario, you would be embodying a positive mindset because you would be putting your best self forward, despite your physical limitations. Having a positive mindset means you can say to yourself, "I tried and I am worthy of trying again. If I continue to show up and provide myself with positivity, I can get closer and closer to reaching my goal each time."

I can imagine you have lots of dreams for yourself and for your family. And maybe you are doing everything right to reach that dream, but the one thing that holds you back is your mindset, where you tell yourself you aren't good enough or you worry that you don't have the right tools. You have the power to change your mindset and to nurture your brain and positivity. Instead of focusing on the negativity in this situation or what could go wrong, focus on what could go right. Visualize your dreams coming true in magnitudes larger than you ever imagined. There will be bumps along the way and your journey will never be a perfect one, but if you believe in yourself, if you trust and believe in the process and if you remember you are capable and worth it, there is no dream too big. A negative mindset may be holding you back, but fostering a positive mindset can help set you free. Visualize your dreams and tell yourself they are possible. You won't always reach your goals, and that's okay, it's part of the process, but positivity allows you to love yourself through the journey toward reaching those goals. If my mom was only positive about the outlook of her life on the days we received good news, I truly believe her journey on this earth would have been shorter. But instead, her motto was to keep positive and to know that she was worthy of continuing to fight for her life. For her, it was about walking into every scan holding onto hope, and using that hope to propel her forward, even if the outcome from the scan was not favorable.

One of the most powerful ways to implement positivity into your day is to practice daily affirmations. Practicing positive affirmations is the first thing I did for myself when I began my healing journey. I knew I needed to learn to love who I was, and learn how to feel beautiful inside and out for me and by me. A positive mindset was the tool that set me free and gave me permission to love

CHAPTER 8 | *LESSON EIGHT*

myself and to find love. My alarm reminded me every morning to write down at least five things in my journal that I loved about myself and five things I was grateful for.

Telling myself I was beautiful every morning even though I felt anything but, was one of the best things I ever did for myself. I started feeding myself with positivity and for the first time in my life, things finally, finally came together. I truly believe without positivity, I would still be in the emotionally abusive relationship I was in and I would still be chasing external validation and missing out on the blessings of my life today. I believe in the power of positivity now more than ever.

I challenge you to do this activity as well and write down what you love about yourself and what you are grateful for. At first, it is likely going to be easier to write down what you are grateful for than it will be to write down positive statements about yourself. It might even feel uncomfortable to write down anything relatively positive about yourself, as it was for me when I first started my self-love journey. With practice, it will feel less uncomfortable and over time your mind and body will begin to believe and embody positivity more easily. Think of your self-love journey as planting seeds. Today, I encourage you to plant just one seed of self-love. I encourage you to think about one positive trait about yourself–maybe you are hard working, or determined, or a great leader, or you are really organized, or a great listener or a great friend, maybe you are kind, or funny, or maybe you have really awesome hair. Plant one seed today of an affirmation for yourself. Planting that seed is the first step to help your tree grow to be full of branches and leaves of self-love affirmations that you can refer back to when you aren't feeling so positive. If you are having a hard time planting that seed and thinking of the first affirmation to start with, I encourage you to ask friends and family what they love about you, and write those affirmations down, even if it feels completely foreign. The continuous act of writing positive statements down in your phone or on paper, and then saying them out loud can help to reframe your mindset.

As you plant your seeds, I want you to take your self-love a step further and begin watering around the seed. You might be struggling to believe the affirmations you are writing down, so it can be really powerful to write the "why" behind each affirmation. For example, if you write down that you are kind, your "why" might be, "I am kind because I enjoy giving compliments" or "I am kind because I always hold the door open for others." Saying the why behind your affirmations can be a great way to demonstrate to yourself that you really do embody that characteristic, just by being the person that you have always been.

I encourage you to start today to plant your seed and water your tree of positive affirmations. Below is an example of how you can write your affirmations every day, but just like we discussed in setting your self-care routine, find what works for you! The first statement in the chart below is an example, and then it will be your turn to fill in your own affirmations. I want you to see just how incredible you are, as you are at this moment.

CHAPTER 8 | *LESSON EIGHT*

Self-Love Affirmations:
I Love Myself Because…

I am determined
Because even when it feels like I have failed, I never give up, I keep trying to reach my goals.

I am _____
Because _____

I am _____
Because _____

I am _____
Because _____

I am _____
Because _____

YOU ARE WORTH FIGHTING FOR

I am so proud of you for starting today to embark on a journey that could change your life for the better. Remember to forgive yourself when you aren't feeling so positive, you are not a failure, you are human. Not every day will be perfect, forgive yourself anyway. Go back to your affirmations and remember how beautiful you are. Remind yourself on the days you feel like you don't like yourself, of all of the reasons you were proud of yourself on prior days. Keep reminding yourself and keep moving forward. Cry about it as much as you need to, but know that your journey is a beautiful one and with hard work you can rise above all that you have been through. One day you will look back and say, "Wow, if I was able to get through that challenging time in the past, then I can get through anything." Continue to find the hope and the light within the darkness. There is joy and hope and light, even on the hardest of days. Tomorrow is never promised for any of us. Today may feel really, really heavy, but there is always, always light, sometimes we just need to look a little bit harder for it. Just like the strength within you, the light is there. The universe is looking out for you, even when it feels like the world is against you. Your truck hasn't come yet, so keep moving forward, and most of all, my mom wants me to remind you to "keep positive."

Lesson Nine

FROM MY MOM

"Pack Your Patience"

CHAPTER 9

YOU ARE A BEAUTIFUL WORK IN PROGRESS

My mom was always my go to person to call on my drives, both long and short. I have a really bad tendency of falling asleep while driving, so having someone on the phone with me, especially on long drives, is helpful to keep my mind busy and keep me awake. My mom was always that person. Somehow we found a way to talk about everything and nothing for hours. Whenever I would find myself stuck in a lot of traffic, I would complain to her about it and she would always say, "Pack your patience." I really needed that reminder because anytime I was in traffic, I was anything but patient. I wanted the traffic to disappear so that I could get to my destination sooner. Similar to being impatient in traffic, we can also often be impatient in our personal lives, wanting instant gratification in all we do.

 As you are reading the pages of this book, you may be thinking of all the steps you want to take to practice self-love, self-compassion and self-care, and you may be hoping that the changes you implement will make you feel better instantly. However, just like when you are in traffic and need to be patient for the traffic to clear, you also have to pack your patience for your mental wellness journey. Most likely you are coming to this book with all kinds of messy baggage, just like the rest of us. For many of us, we will spend the rest of our lives unpacking that messy baggage, and that's okay. You have years and years of unlearning to do and years and years of potential trauma and hardships to unpack, and that takes time. The fact that it takes time is not to discourage you from ever starting your mental wellness journey, but instead, I want it to encourage you to know that this journey is messy, but the journey is worth it because you are a beautiful and constant work in progress. Traffic takes time to clear out, and once it has cleared, you are able to get back on track at a smooth pace to your destination. The same applies to your mental wellness journey. You are embarking on a journey that takes time to clear out and work through all of the past pains, traumas and negativities you have experienced. With some work, patience, kindness, self-love and self-compassion, you can begin to work through the past, and continue your journey forward.

As you pack your patience on this journey, you will experience both good and bad times. Just like any trip you take in the future, there will be traffic you will encounter, and you will also encounter more bumps in your mental health journey. The journey is not perfect and it can be really, really challenging. It can also be really frustrating when you feel like you have gotten to a great point in your mental health journey–where you feel like you have worked through a lot of past traumas and feel secure in yourself and who you are and are doing great practicing self-care– and despite all of that, the traffic of life comes knocking at your

CHAPTER 9 | *LESSON NINE*

door and a new struggle awaits you. This new struggle may stop you in your tracks and may make you doubt yourself, despite all of the self-love work you have done. This new struggle may make you feel anxious or depressed or make you feel isolated from the people who you usually rely on. This new struggle may bring up past traumas that you thought you had worked through. This is why it is so important to pack your patience and to have patience with the process of mental health recovery as well as with yourself. Mental health recovery is not going to be linear. We are going to have challenges in our lives, but those challenges only help us to grow in strength and resiliency for future difficult times. It's okay to struggle again with things that you have struggled with in the past. It's truly okay to not be okay. Mental wellness is a lifelong journey. When we can accept that, it makes the journey easier, because instead of getting angry with ourselves for having a "setback," we can be patient with ourselves and realize that tough times are inevitable, but we have the self-care tools within us and the resources and supports around us to help us to keep moving forward. When you can accept that your mental wellness journey is a lifelong one, you can give yourself grace when tough times come your way.

I remember about a year after starting therapy, I felt like I had recovered. I was in a much better space mentally and was feeling secure in my self-love journey. My therapist also agreed that it was okay for me to stop therapy because of how well I was doing. Shortly after stopping, I felt myself slipping into deep anxious thoughts and I knew I needed to start therapy back up again. Feelings of insecurity, pain from my last relationship, fears and sadness around past traumas, and struggling with maintaining my newfound sense of self-love were all reasons that propelled me to return to therapy. Restarting therapy or any other mental health tool does not make you a failure, just like you are not a failure if you have to start going to the gym again, or restart your tutoring sessions or restart working toward a degree. You are not a failure if you struggle in the future or have to restart, you are human, experiencing challenges day to day, week to week, year to year, just like me, just like all of us. By taking this time to work on your mental wellness and give yourself the tools and love you need from yourself and from the resources around you, you are giving yourself a strong foundation that will allow you to see a challenge, allow yourself to feel the sadness around that challenge, and then remind yourself that you have gotten through tough times in the past and you will do so again and again. It's important to remind yourself to pack your patience in all experiences that are challenging.

As you pack your patience for your mental wellness journey, it's also important to pause on this trip of life and be thankful for all that you have endured because of the growth it has given to you. I think a lot of this is due to the fact that we go through our lives looking for instant gratification. We think about our dreams and how amazing they would be if they turned out to be exactly how we want them to be, but when we realize those dreams will take time to accomplish, we get discouraged and disheartened. We don't congratulate ourselves for even having that idea, and we often don't feel good about the small win we accomplished. While we might never fully get our instant gratification mindsets to go away, we can be realistic with ourselves about our goals and celebrate our growth. When we can do that, we can be grateful for the journey, even if it is a slow one. No matter how slow the growth is, there is growth, and that growth is beautiful. So instead of getting frustrated with yourself for falling short or not reaching your goal as quickly as you wanted, stop and pause and be proud of yourself for doing more than you were doing yesterday. Be thankful for the growth you have made with every step. Instead of seeking out instant gratification, focus on having long lasting gratitude for the journey you are continuously growing on.

All of your experiences to this date have allowed you to grow into the very person you are today. We all still have a long way to go, and we will never be perfect, which is not the goal anyway, but we are stronger today in this moment than we ever have been before. Even if at this moment, you feel weak or discouraged, you have done so much up until this point, and you have everything within you to get through this difficult time. You have grown, and just like a flower you will bloom. You will use your experiences of the past, no matter how sad, traumatic, or hurtful they might have been, to propel you forward. It can be so helpful to pause in your pursuit of happiness, success, or love, and just be grateful that you are who you are, and that you have been where you have been. Because without those experiences, you wouldn't be here today, strong in your foundation, ready to take the world by storm, knowing that no matter how long the journey is to your goal, your strength will grow.

The next time you feel stuck in a struggle or the next time you are feeling down on yourself because you feel like you've taken steps back in your mental wellness journey, where you were doing so well and now you can barely get out of bed, remind yourself to pack your patience. Remind yourself that you are worthy of experiencing patience on this journey. You are not going to figure out all of your mental health problems overnight. It takes time to figure out what self-care tools work for you, how you're going to implement those tools into your daily routine and who is in your support system that you feel confident to reach out to. It takes time to work through the stigma you have believed your entire life to even reach out for the help that you know you need. It takes time to work through years of negative self-talk to even begin to believe positive affirmations about yourself. It takes time to rewire your brain from the anxious thoughts that have kept you from reaching your goals.

There is no set time for when you will feel better or when you will rewire your negative thoughts, but I think that's what makes this journey of self-love special. Because along the way, you will learn so much about yourself and you will know that although you may encounter challenges, there is always hope, even when you feel the long hours of work that you have put in for your self-care and self-love have become unraveled by that challenge. All of those long hours have not disappeared now that you are in a new struggle. The work you put in will be with you for the rest of your life. The work you invested into yourself has provided the strongest foundation for you. You can look back and ask yourself, "What tools did I use or who did I reach out to when I struggled the last time? What worked for me then? How can I reuse those tools for this situation? How can I find mindful moments in this situation? Who can I reach out to that made me feel comforted last time in a similar situation? What self-care tools can I add into my current routine for a boost of self-care? How can I make time for myself in this situation?" Because you have done the work, you now have the tools to even ask yourself these questions and you can validate your own experiences and allow yourself to truly feel your feelings, rather than brushing them off as insignificant. Because you have done the work, you can remind yourself that you will come out on the other side, even if it is a long and difficult journey. Because you've done the work, you can be patient with yourself if you stopped practicing self-care or if your current self-care routine no longer works. You are doing the work, and that is going to help to propel you forward. So be proud of yourself that you are planting your self-care and self-love seed and no matter what obstacles you may encounter, you have the foundation and tools to pack your patience and hold onto hope that you can get through this.

Pack your patience today and every day. You are doing the best you can with the situation you have, and that is more than enough. Traffic and hard times are inevitable, but we can be patient with ourselves on this journey and love ourselves through it, and that's beautiful.

FROM MY MOM

"A Place For Everything And Everything In Its Place"

CHAPTER 10

EVEN WHEN YOU FEEL LOST, YOU CAN ALWAYS FIND YOURSELF AGAIN

Similar to my mom's lesson of "organization is the key to life," she would tell us over and over, "A place for everything and everything in its place," especially when we couldn't find something that was not where it was supposed to be. Everything should have a place that it will live in order to stay organized, and that way when you are looking for it, you know exactly where it will be. When you don't put that item away in the right spot, or don't put it away at all, you might lose it and not be able to find it when you go looking for it in the spot it is supposed to be. In a lot of cases, however, the item you were looking for, shows up, it just might take longer to find it than had it been in its place. This same lesson can be applied to our feelings of losing our sense of self and feeling out of place.

If you ever experience a situation where you feel like you have lost yourself, you might struggle to find yourself again. Maybe you've lost a big part of your identity. Maybe you are an athlete and you've been injured and you can no longer compete. Or maybe you fill your identity with social activities and something like a pandemic takes away your ability to interact with others. Maybe you have taken on one too many roles and you are overwhelmed and have lost sight of the things you used to do that made you feel like yourself. I have been there before, especially in the last year of losing my mom, I also simultaneously felt like I lost myself. I had to remind myself that feeling lost was only a season of my life, it didn't have to be permanent, and that I could eventually find myself again or even reinvent myself. I had to be intentional about being patient and calm with myself in my grieving journey as I was not only grieving the loss of my mom but also the loss of a big part of myself. I was intentional about creating slow and mindful spaces for myself throughout my days and giving myself whatever I needed that day, whether it was more rest, more time in the sunshine, time away from social media on hard days like Mother's Day, or time to meet up with a friend who I knew would make me laugh. Creating these intentional spaces allowed me to find myself again and allowed me to create a slightly different version of myself that is even kinder to myself than I was before, a version of myself that only chooses to do tasks and activities that are fulfilling for me, because I have realized that life is too short to do anything that robs you of your joy. I created a place for my mental health, just like we create places and spaces for the items we own.

    Just like me, you, too, can find yourself again if you feel like you've lost yourself. As the pages before have reminded you, you have done so much work already for your mental health and you continue to do so much work for your mental health. I promise that even if you feel lost, the core of your goals, desires, dreams, strengths and knowledge is still inside of you, growing every day, even when it doesn't feel like it. You may find a new version of yourself that may take a while to get to know, but the core of you and your motivation, desires, joy for life and happiness, is still inside you. It may take time to really feel those feelings again, but when you do, I hope you give yourself love and compassion and know that you may lose yourself again, but you can always, always be found.

My mom would tell you that the best way to find a place for your mental health is to have a place for everything and everything in its place, so that you can easily find the tools you used before in the past. Here are some ways you can find a place for your mental wellness tools:

- Write down your positive affirmations and gratitude statements and hang them above your bed so you see them every morning when you wake up as a reminder of the beautiful person you are and the beautiful people and opportunities around you.
- Mark the contacts in your phone who have been your key supporters and accountability partners as your favorites or put them on speed dial so you can easily reach out to them when you need support or a listening ear.
- Make a list of your self-care tools and put them in your phone and create reminders and alerts on your phone to practice those tools.

The more mental health practices you can have organized and in a specific place, the easier it will be to find them when you are feeling lost, overwhelmed or down. Create space for your mental wellness in your life and create a place for it to exist in your life. Create a place for your mental wellness tools that is easy for you to access, so that even when you are at your lowest, you can always find the tools that work for you. Even if you lose your mental wellness tools because you have forgotten them, stopped practicing them for a while, or truly lost the paper full of affirmations, rest assured that you can always start again and reach out for help to an accountability partner, a friend, or a therapist to remind yourself of the tools you can use to begin taking care of you and loving you, as you are again. You can always come back to the pages of this book and the lessons from my mom for your mental wellness, that can help you to start this journey again. Just like the keys you lost because they were supposed to be in the key bowl but in a rush were quickly tossed on the couch, which you later found, you will find yourself again, it might just take a little extra time, effort and patience.

If you are struggling in any way with relationships, with losing your sense of self, with your confidence, with staying motivated to do the things you used to love to do, or with anything else, this is your reminder that it is okay to feel that way. If you're struggling to find the passion around things that used to get you fired up and excited, I feel you and see you and you are not alone. If you do not have energy toward your responsibilities because your energy is going toward your grief or pain, remember that it is okay for priorities to shift. Things change, we change, we grow, our perspectives and our desires and needs change. This change does not make you a failure. Hold onto hope that although change is inevitable, it isn't all bad, and that whatever storm you are on, it will pass and only make you stronger and more resilient. We might have to start again, we might feel helpless and upset, but we have the power and strength to try over and over. I think that is really powerful, to be able to say, "This is really hard, but I know I can get through this and that I can try again."

Oftentimes, when I've lost something like my keys or an important document, I come back to this lesson from my mom. I quietly center myself and ask her to send me a sign of where that item is hiding. It takes a while, but eventually, the item catches my eye and I feel at peace that I have it back in my posession. It's the same with finding ourselves. Take that quiet moment of reflection when you are feeling lost, angry, sad, overwhelmed or stressed out to find your own sense of peace and calm and then ask yourself where are the tools and resources you have used in the past that you can pull out now for this unique situation. Everything has a place, even when it's lost, it can be found–just like you, just like your mental wellness journey. No matter how frustrating or overwhelming this journey may be, you are worthy of the journey, there is hope in the journey, and you will end up exactly where you are supposed to be, maybe not how you planned, but likely even better than you could have imagined. Trust the journey and find a place for your mental wellness in your daily life and always know you can come back when you need to, you are deserving of that.

Lesson Eleven

FROM MY MOM AND HER FINAL REMINDER

"This Too Shall Pass"

CHAPTER

KEEP MOVING FORWARD

My mom passed away one week after I found out that I was pregnant. I had always dreamed of my mom being a grandmother and I talked about it often with her and with others. That one week of my mom knowing that I was pregnant was the closest thing I got to her actually being a grandmother here on earth. That week was quick and it wasn't the grandmother experience I had always dreamed of, but it was still really magical to see the joy, wonder, and possibility on her face. There's so many questions that I wish I could have asked my mom about pregnancy, babies and motherhood, but in one of our final conversations, I did get to ask her what her biggest piece of motherly advice would be. She told me that motherhood is difficult, (which it is) and that there would be times when I would be really, really frustrated (and she was right) but she also reminded me that despite all the ups and downs of motherhood, that it would be important for me to remind myself that **this too shall pass**. I hold onto that final reminder from my mom every day. Although this lesson was not one my mom said often or one that she created herself, she left me with a final lesson of knowledge and peace that keeps me going every day. It was her reminder that even when life got hard, there would always be light on the other side.

As we come to the end of this journey together in this book, I want to remind you as well, that this too shall pass–whatever you are going through, will pass. It feels heavy and sad and dark right now, and I get that, but don't stop fighting for yourself. **You are and have always been worth fighting for.** This unimaginably hard time will pass. I know it doesn't feel like it will at this moment, but it will. And one day you will look back and be proud of yourself for fighting for you and choosing you every single day, even when it felt difficult to do so. This too shall pass–just keep holding on for another day. Sometimes taking things one day at a time is even too much, so take things one hour or even one moment or even one task at a time. It may feel impossible, but you can and you will get through it. As you reflect on your journey and the lessons you have learned in your own life and throughout these chapters, really ask yourself right now what you need or who you can surround yourself with, in order to work through this challenge.

Can you believe how far we have come together on this journey? There are tears streaming down my face right now as I write this final chapter. The one thing that keeps me moving forward in this life is knowing how proud my mom would be of me right now, and I just know she is beaming down from heaven with joy that I finally wrote this book and that it honors her life and legacy. I am also so proud of you for sticking with me and getting this far. You should be proud of yourself, too. You set on this journey of the unknown. You stepped out of your comfort zone, simply by opening this book and continuing to turn the pages. I am so proud of you for fighting through the pain and for continuing to move forward, despite all of the days you didn't think you could keep going. I am proud of you for choosing you, even when other choices seemed more desirable. I am proud of you for choosing to see the light within the darkness; for choosing to not settle; for choosing to be who you are, despite what others think; for asking for help and seeking out that help; and for just getting through another minute, when getting through the day feels impossible. You have fought through difficult times and moved forward and continued to show up for yourself even when you didn't want to. You have continuously kept going and have continued to put one foot in front of the other. I want you to be proud of yourself, because you truly have done what once felt unthinkable and impossible. You are here another day. You are doing something right now that a year ago, or even a day ago, felt like it would never happen. You are growing, molding, changing and becoming the person you were meant to be. You are learning tools to work through future tough days. You are growing in your strength and resiliency.

Whatever lessons you have taken from this book, bring them with you everywhere you go. I hope the next time you are in traffic, you remind yourself to *pack your patience*, and use that as a time to reflect on how you can also be more patient with yourself in the constant tug and pull of challenges and healing that you will experience in your life. I hope you know that *you can do bad all by yourself*, and that you don't have to stay in a relationship or job or friendship that doesn't serve you, grow you, or make you happy. I hope you know that external validation will always feel good, but I hope you realize that you don't need to depend on that external validation, and that learning to validate yourself is a beautiful gift. I hope you can *look at yourself as a third person* and give yourself the same love, respect, kindness and compassion that you so easily give to others. I hope you choose to *keep positive* and to find the light even in the darkest of times. I hope you know that you can take care of your mental health like you would *take care of your teeth* and to *be your own superhero*, too. I hope you remember that *organization is the key to life* as you set your self-care schedule and routine and find what works for you. I hope you know that *there's a place for everything and everything in its place*, including tools for your mental health, and that even when we have lost ourselves, we can begin again and be found. I hope you know it's always okay to feel your feelings and that what you are going through is always valid, no matter what anyone else thinks or no matter how much the stigma around mental health tries to put you down, because at the end of the day, *it's better to be pissed off than to be pissed on*. I hope you know that even if you've made mistakes in the past or if you fall back on your self-care routine, *you don't have to be sorry about it, but you can be conscious* about using the lessons from your mistakes to propel you forward. I hope that if you ever buy a house, that you know you are worthy of having *nothing less than a bath and a half* so you don't have to impatiently wait your turn to use the bathroom, but that you also always remember that you are worthy of going after your dreams and learning to love yourself as you are in this moment. I hope you find your bath and a half. I hope you find your worth. I hope you love yourself so fiercely that you can be compassionate with yourself even when you do not feel so in love with yourself. I hope when you fall down, you know you can always get back up and that you are surrounded by so many people to help lift you higher

CHAPTER 11 | *LESSON ELEVEN*

and that you always remember that *this too shall pass*. I hope you know that this journey is not easy and that it's messy and confusing, but it's worth it, because you are worth it. My mom would want all of that for you, just like she wants it for me.

Although life is full of ups and downs, good times and bad, it is within each of those moments that we learn more about ourselves, that we become more forgiving and patient with ourselves, and that we recognize each moment, no matter how wonderful and life changing or how painful and scary, is a moment of our story. A beautiful story that is unique to you. A story that shows your inner and outer shine. A story of growth and hope. Always remember who you are is a gift. You are a gift to this world just by being you. Give yourself credit for all you have done and know that you are on this earth for a reason. You have purpose, talent, beauty, and so much more to share with the world and there are so many people who love you for exactly who you are, despite your flaws. You may not believe it, but every moment you walk this earth, you add something to it that wouldn't have existed had you not been here. **How incredible is that? To realize that the world is better, because you are in it.** I hope you are able to put yourself first and give yourself the gift of self-love, the gift of feeling your feelings, the gift of practicing self-care and seeking help, and the gift of choosing yourself again and again, even when it is messy or confusing.

I am so proud of you. And I am so proud of myself. Because at one point, I didn't think I would be living the life I am living, or living a life at all. But here I am, just like you, figuring it out with every step, and choosing me even when things are uncertain. Keep choosing you. Keep moving forward even when the going gets tough. You have done it so many times before, you already have all the tools within you to do it again.

Let's keep fighting for ourselves, together.

Appendix

Resources:

NATIONAL SUICIDE PREVENTION LIFELINE
- 24/7, toll-free hotline available to aid anyone in suicidal crisis, anyone having a tough time mentally, or anyone having a bad day. There is someone to talk to you. Dial 988. (Just like you'd dial 911.)

CRISIS TEXT LINE
- Text HOME to 741741 for 24/7 support for the struggle with suicidal thoughts or a bad day. If texting feels like a better way to get support, this is the resource for you!

PSYCHOLOGY TODAY
- Find a therapist (psychologytoday.com) in your area! Filter on insurance, area of focus, type of therapy,

demographics of therapist, and more to find the perfect therapist for you!

TALKSPACE
- Online therapy and support. Send a therapist text messages, audio messages, as well as picture and video messages in a private, text-based chat room.

NATIONAL SEXUAL ASSAULT HOTLINE
- Call 800.656.HOPE (4673) to be connected with a trained staff member from a sexual assault service provider in your area.

SAMHSA'S LIFELINE
- Free, confidential, 24/7 treatment referral and information service (in English and Spanish) for individuals and families facing mental and/or substance use disorders. Call 1-800-662-HELP (4357)

NAMI LIFELINE
- Free peer-support service providing information, resource referrals and support to people living with a mental health conditions, their family members and caregivers, mental health providers and the public. The NAMI HelpLine can be reached Monday through Friday, 10 am–6 pm, ET. 1-800-950-NAMI (6264) or info@nami.org.

MY3 APP

- MY3 lets you stay connected when you are struggling. With MY3, you define your network and your plan to stay safe. Download MY3 to make sure that your three are there to help you when you need them most.

THERAPY FOR BLACK MEN

- The stigma around mental health for men is incredibly high, especially for black men. You don't have to "man up," you can get help. This provides resources to find a therapist and coach for mental wellness.

THERAPY FOR BLACK GIRLS

- Connect with other women of color for support, find therapists of color in your area, and access to a podcast and other resources!

TREVOR PROJECT

- The Trevor Project is a great resource for LGBTQ youth. The Trevor Project has trained counselors for support 24/7. If you are struggling or need a safe space to talk, you can call the TrevorLifeline 24/7 at 1-866-488-7386. There is also a live chat, as well as "TrevorSpace" which is a social networking site for lesbian, gay, bisexual, transgender, queer and questioning (LGBTQ) youth under 25 and their friends and allies.

HEADSPACE APP

- Learn to meditate with Headspace!

SHINE APP
- Created by women of color for all of us. A tool to create a daily self-care ritual. Guided meditations and support.

Acknowledgements

So many people to thank for the creation of this book!

My biggest thank you to my mom, my forever best friend, who has always encouraged me to write this book, believed in me, even when I didn't believe in myself, and continues to shine down on me from heaven. Mom, we did it! Without you and your witty sayings, there would be no book, so thank you. I'll always be looking for the purple in my life, your favorite color and the color for Pancreatic Cancer Awareness. I miss you, your light and your love beyond words. I love you more. Thank you to my dad, who has always pushed me to go after my dreams and who reminds me every day how proud my mom would be of me. Thank you for reminding me over and over that I was capable of writing this book. To my daughter, Charlotte, I wouldn't get through my days without you and your beautiful smile, you have healed me in more ways than you will ever know. Thank you for teaching me patience and the greatest love I've ever known. Thank you to my Aunt Shirley, who has stepped up for me in so many ways since my mom passed away. You were the first person to read my entire book in the early stages, and that just shows me how much you love me. I know you are always just one call away and I appreciate all of the support (and laughter) you continuously give me. Thank you to my Aunt Mary - you have always called just to see how I am doing and you always validate my ideas and provide strength when I need it. Thanks for reminding me to "hang tough." Thank you to my brother, Dion, whose support of my dreams does not go unnoticed.

Thank you to my incredible friends who have cheered me on throughout this entire journey and have also helped me so much in my grieving journey. Avery for always knowing exactly what to say, Laura for the decades of validation and unwavering love and so many funny voice notes, Maria for always cheering me on and reminding me to advocate for what I need, Amy for always, always checking in and for the wonderful idea of purple flowers, Tiara for the continuous acknowledgement, Danielle for the laughs that keep me going, Melanie for always being here even after lapses in time, Amanda for being by my side through track years and beyond, and Ato for laughing at my jokes and always making me feel like I can conquer the world - you all are my rocks, I'd be lost without you all. Thank you to Asia, Sumia and Ashley for doing mom life with me and for your constant understanding, validation and love. You all make the tough days a lot easier.

Thank you to Anke for marking the start of my therapy journey and helping me redefine who Ivy is. My story of healing wouldn't exist without you. Thank you to Jules and Tara, for your guidance and support during each new chapter of my life.

Thank you to every school I have worked with in the past and every student, coach, parent or educator that I have spoken to.

ACKNOWLEDGEMENTS

Each of you have played a role in inspiring me to continue to do the work that I do every day. To Kaytie, Magali and Shanesha at WPY - you allowed me to set my wings free and gave me the space to write this book, so I ultimately can spend even more time with my sweet girl - thank you.

A special thank you to Geo Derice, my "book doula" who has mentored me throughout this entire process and really gave me the push to finally start this book. You truly are a gem, Geo (see my reference there?! Check out his book, *Geo's Gems*!!) Thank you to Charlotte's babysitter, Bryanna, your visits once a week during this process have helped me to be able to hold this book in my hands.

Thank you to PanCAN, for your tireless efforts to find a cure for pancreatic cancer and for always sharing my mom's story.

Lastly, I want to thank my book editor, Jessica Gang, cover designer, Tri Widyatmaka, interior book designer, Honeylette, and amazing photographer, Molly Greeley. You all gave this book its beautiful final touches.

About The Author

Ivy Watts, MPH, is a sought out Mental Health Empowerment Speaker, entrepreneur, and also the founder of her mental wellness blog, *Beautifully Simply You*. Ivy is a former All-American track and field student-athlete and a Top 30 Finalist for the NCAA Woman of the Year Award Throughout her life, she appeared to have it all together, yet struggled with her mental health and self-worth in silence. Ivy now strives to break the stigma around mental health by sharing her struggle with her mental health through the various stages of her life, as well as her tools for overall mental wellness. Ivy has spoken to and empowered tens of thousands of students, student-athletes, coaches, educators, administrators and parents to learn the power of self-love, self-care and mental wellness. Ivy has also hosted first-of its-kind, city-wide Mental Health Awareness Events that have raised awareness and reduced mental health stigma.

Ivy has her undergraduate degree in Psychology from University of New Haven and her Masters in Public Health from

Boston University. She is also certified in Mental Health First Aid. Ivy was born and raised in Boston, Massachusetts and currently lives there with her daughter Charlotte Sang.

If you are interested in having Ivy come and speak to your group, you can learn more about her speaking topics at ivywattsspeaks.com and contact her at ivy@ivywattsspeaks.com. If you'd like to read Ivy's blogs (new blogs are posted twice a month) for even more self-care and mental wellness, head to beautifullysimplyyou.com.

www.ingramcontent.com/pod-product-compliance
Lightning Source LLC
Chambersburg PA
CBHW032052150426
43194CB00006B/506